D1561928

RING AROUND MAX

THE CORRESPONDENCE OF
RING LARDNER & MAX PERKINS

**Edited by
CLIFFORD M. CARUTHERS**

NORTHERN ILLINOIS UNIVERSITY PRESS

DeKalb, Illinois

Library of Congress Cataloging in Publication Data

Lardner, Ring Wilmer, 1885-1933.
   Ring around Max.

   "A chronological listing of first publications
of Ring Lardner's book and magazine pieces":   p.
    I.   Perkins, Maxwell Evarts, 1884-1947.
II.   Caruthers, Clifford M., 1935-   ed.   III.   Title.
PS3523.A7Z54   1973   818'.5'209 [B]   72-6919
ISBN 0-87580-041-6
ISBN 0-87580-512-4 (pbk)

Printed in the United States of America

CONTENTS

PREFACE

The editorial policy adopted in this book has been to present a diplomatic transcription, reproducing the letters as exactly as possible, with the following exceptions. Lardner's oddities in type-spacing—he frequently omits spaces after commas and periods—have been ignored, and all closing signatures have been omitted. Letterheads, addresses, dates, salutations, and complimentary closes have been typographically stylized by the publisher; Perkins always writes from his New York office. "*Sic's*" have not been used. All existing correspondence between the two has been included, with interstitial commentary to provide transitions where needed and to amplify the subjects at hand. Briefer explanatory footnotes on persons, places, and things appear at the bottoms of pages.

I wish to thank the Deans' Fund Grants Board of Northern Illinois University for financial assistance and the Princeton University Library for access to the Charles Scribner's Sons Archives. I am most grateful to Ring Lardner, Jr., and to Charles Scribner's Sons for permission to publish these letters, title pages, and the photographs of Lardner and Perkins. The book is dedicated to all my past teachers.

26 September 1972   C.M.C.
DeKalb, Illinois

FOREWORD

The biggest names in the American literary world of the 1920s were Fitzgerald, Hemingway, Wolfe, and Maxwell Perkins, the editor who published them all at Charles Scribner's Sons. These men appear to have dominated the scene, because their goals were high and their achievements substantial. But the majority of Americans then, as now, read their newspapers and magazines much more often than they patronized bookstores, and the writers with whom they came into contact daily were of more interest to them. The greatest of newspaper columnists at that time was Ring Lardner. His name was a household word throughout the country from 1919, when he began to write for the Bell Syndicate, until his death in 1933. In the columns, articles, and stories he published in such quality magazines as the *Saturday Evening Post, Cosmopolitan, Liberty,* and the *New Yorker,* Lardner spoke to these everyday people in their own language, and they listened; by 1923 Lardner was unquestionably one of the ten best-known names in America. These average citizens also sensed—better than most of the reigning literary critics who could not readily believe in a "half-educated" midwesterner's stories of the baseball diamond and the petty concerns of bourgeois life—that Lardner was truly a first-rate artist. His readers knew the accuracy of his fictional world as well as that of his language, and they reacted with an enthusiasm no publisher could ignore.

Thus Maxwell Perkins came onto the scene. Urged by Fitzgerald, who campaigned as strenuously for Lardner as he did later for Hemingway, Perkins read Lardner's magazine stories and recognized his great literary talent. The Perkins-Lardner correspondence is the record of Lardner's emergence, as a result, from writer to author, from merely a popular columnist to a recognized satirist and incisive depictor of the comedy and depravity of the populace. It is an emergence which Perkins accomplished, moreover, only with great difficulty, for Lardner clearly had no passionate interest in having his work collected into books. It is clear from these letters that, after 1923, the motivating force behind the publication of Lardner's books was always Maxwell Perkins, who selected the contents from Lardner's magazine publications, suggested format, chapter and sometimes book titles, offered plots, at times even tactfully reworked the text, and always encouraged Lardner to write more fiction, and especially to write the novel Perkins thought he could do, but which Lardner for various reasons never got around to writing.

Prominent in the background of this correspondence is Scott Fitzgerald. He was, from the time he became Lardner's neighbor in Great Neck, in October 1922, Lardner's close friend and perhaps greatest admirer. Fitzgerald, however, deplored Lardner's apparent lack of regard for his talent and lack of desire to achieve a serious reputation as a writer of fiction. The first letter in the correspondence, expressing Scribner's interest in publishing a collection of Lardner's stories, is the direct result of Fitzgerald's enthusiastic recommendation to Perkins. And there are many references to Zelda and Scott Fitzgerald in this correspondence, ranging from inquiries about their health and states of mind to significant comments about the quality and the sales of Fitzgerald's books.

In 1923, when Perkins at Fitzgerald's urging wrote the initial letter to Lardner, he had been with Scribner's already for thirteen years. He was hired first as advertising manager, and became an editor in 1914. From the beginning, he consistently exerted all his influence toward the development of a more liberal publishing policy by his old-guard, conservative publishing house toward the relatively unrestrained writing of the World War I era and the 1920s. Charles Scribner, for example, had to be convinced of Lardner's literary merit before the "slangy sports writer" could be brought into the Scribner's fold.

A New Englander educated at Harvard, Perkins was by nature conservative, disciplined, persevering, and tough-minded. Chard Powers Smith, speaking of his impressions during a first meeting in 1930, described Perkins's physical appearance as that of a

> middle-sized man on the lean or stringy side, light-boned, wiry, long-necked and Adam's appled; well tailored in gray; the hair hay-color drying towards gray on the sides; the complexion weathered smooth like a piece of old barn siding; the nose strong and severe in lines but delicate in texture, like skin stretched over china, obviously a mark of breeding; the gentle speech, equally high New York and high Boston; the hands and gestures with a feminine sensitivity but without effeminacy; the expression—in this first interview— mostly the plain stare looking away from me, garnished occasionally by the flash of appraisal and often by an easy smile which was not typical and was simply his social manner with a stranger; altogether a semi-rustic fusion of toughness and great gentleness such as only New England could produce out of ten or a dozen generations, a figure that would be easy in bared suspenders with a pitchfork on top of a hayload, and just as easy in a cutaway with a silk hat and a gold-headed cane.

By 1930, largely as a result of Perkins's ability to cajole the best out of his writers and his uncanny recognition of quality, Scribner's had become the acknowledged hub of American literary activity. In addition to Fitzgerald, Lardner, Hemingway, and Wolfe, the firm published during this time the books of such diverse contemporaries as Stark Young, Struthers Burt, James Boyd, S. S. Van Dine, Marjorie Rawlings, Conrad Aiken, Christine Weston, Will James, and Arthur Train. Perhaps Perkins's perception of quality was due to the new philosophy of publishing which he articulated, on one occasion, to a prospective writer (whose novel about an editor Perkins had declined to publish):

> Then, in the end, you have your editor go out for himself as a publisher, on the basis of certain resolutions. One of these is, to my mind, a complete betrayal of his profession—that he will only publish books which will coincide with his own views. If he is that kind of man, let him speak for himself and be a writer. But the function of a publisher in society is to furnish a means by which anyone of a certain level of intelligence and abilities can express his views. A publisher should not be, as such, a partisan, however strongly partisan he may be as an individual. If he allows his partisanship to govern him in his choice of books, he is a traitor to the public. He is supposed to furnish a forum for the free play of the intellect, in so far as he possibly can.

Perkins's prime criterion for an author was talent, regardless of how deeply he might disapprove of the author's ideas or style. And it was Perkins's ability to discern real talent, along with his capacities to handle the needs and personalities of different authors, which was primarily responsible for his great success as an editor. In the area of perceiving talent, John Hall Wheelock, his successor as editor-in-chief at Scribner's, referred to Perkins's ability as an "intuitive perceptivity that was uncanny." Moreover, Perkins was flexible enough to assume different roles with different writers. To Thomas Wolfe, from whose voluminous manuscripts Perkins extracted the published novels, Perkins became not only the close friend and advisor Wolfe needed (he was, later, even Wolfe's literary executor) but also virtually a co-author, to the extent that Wolfe eventually switched to Harper & Bros. in a desperate effort to prove to the world that he could write his own novels. To Hemingway, Perkins astutely demonstrated his respect for the Hemingway mystique of the big game hunter and general sportsman. To Fitzgerald, Perkins was, as revealed in the *Dear Scott/Dear Max* correspondence recently published by Scribner's, not only a perceptive editor but also a personal advisor, friend, and paternal figure for the sensitive, unstable Fitzgerald. Such success in the publication of the most prominent American literary writers of the 1920s made Scribner's a kind of congregative center of American literature at that time and Maxwell Perkins the man actually in control of that literary renaissance. Perkins became vice-president of Scribner's and editor-in-chief in 1932, and, by the time of his death, 17 June 1947, probably had had more books dedicated to him than has any other American in this century.

But the master was very nearly stumped by Lardner's lack of enthusiasm. In fact, Perkins found that Lardner had not even retained copies of his own stories after they had been published in the *Saturday Evening Post, Cosmopolitan, McClures,* and other popular periodicals; Perkins himself had to obtain back copies of these magazines before *How to Write Short Stories* could be collected and published. Unlike Fitzgerald or Wolfe, who depended heavily upon their books for a livelihood, Lardner had made a conscious commitment to earning his living and reputation primarily as a columnist rather than as a literary writer. During the twenties, Lardner earned up to $30,000 annually from his Bell Syndicate column, and supplemented this income by as much as another $25,000 a year from his work in the theater and in Ziegfeld's Follies, and from the publication of his fiction in periodicals.

His stories were much in demand: he eventually obtained the top price from the *Post,* which was then $1250 a story, and he received as much as $3500 for each story accepted by *Cosmopolitan*. It seems clear that although Lardner was pleased to have his stories collected and published in book form—and to be generally well received by such critics as Mencken, Seldes, Van Doren, and Cowley as a significant writer of serious fiction—he made a conscious choice to opt for immediate money rather than for the uncertain royalties and literary reputation that Scribner's offered him. This correspondence makes that attitude quite clear, but this is not to say that Lardner did not care about the quality of his work. Ring, Jr., in his March 1972 *Esquire* article, "Ring Lardner and Sons," emphasizes that while his father cared a great deal about the value of what he wrote he never exhibited a strong ambition to become known as a serious writer of fiction. Instead, he appears to have elected to be the best breadwinner he could be. The implications of this correspondence thus tend to refute in part the myth expressed by such writers as Mencken, Dreiser, and Lewis that the America of the 1920s was so materialistic that it tended to crush talents such as Lardner's. Lardner obviously had opportunity and great encouragement from Perkins, and perhaps could have written the novel Perkins wanted if he had chosen to allocate his time and priorities differently. But even later in his career, when his financial condition was secure, Lardner preferred, again consciously, to devote himself primarily to musical comedy and theater (his first love) rather than to serious prose fiction. Nevertheless, the fiction he did produce achieves a strikingly high quality.

In 1923, when Perkins made his initial offer, Lardner was widely known as a sports writer but was not regarded as a writer of serious fiction. He had acquired this reputation chiefly through his column "In the Wake of the News" (3 June 1913-20 June 1919 for the *Chicago Tribune*) and subsequently through his Bell Syndicate column. George Doran had published *You Know Me Al*, the epistles of the fictional Jack Keefe, in 1916; Bobbs-Merrill had published *Gullible's*

Travels. The Young Immigrunts, and a number of other minor books before 1923; but Lardner had received little critical attention before Perkins published him at Scribner's. With the publication of *How to Write Short Stories* (1924), *The Love Nest and Other Stories* (1926), and *Round Up* (1929), Lardner emerged as a significant humorist and satirist with a keen "philological" ear for American dialects. This achievement has seemed astonishing to many who have dismissed Lardner as a provincial, half-educated writer. But actually Lardner's education was considerably better than average (his vocabulary, for instance, when he does not choose to write in dialect, reveals a rather learned diction and a superior command of the classics). Though he attended college only one semester (at the Armour Institute in Chicago, where he excelled in rhetoric and failed everything else), his early education in the home (he did not attend elementary school) was exceptional. The Lardner home in Niles, Michigan, was, chiefly as a result of his mother's reputation as a local poetess, the literary center of the town. This early training, together with his observations early in his newspaper career, when he was a traveling reporter with both the Chicago Cubs and the White Sox, led to the development not only of a keen ear for the spoken language but also to an excellent understanding of the common American.

In all, Lardner wrote only about a hundred short stories, but probably no other modern American writer, except perhaps Hemingway, has been imitated so much. And even Hemingway once referred to himself as an "early imitator and always admirer" of Ring Lardner. Mencken, particularly, in the early 1920s, and many other critics later, praised Lardner's re-creation of the diction and the rhythms of American dialogue. Occasionally, as in the story "Women," this dialogue is simply a careful rendering of the language of the baseball dugout:

> "Look at that!" interrupted Young Jake, his eyes on the field of action. "What could Sam of been thinkin'!"
>
> "Thinkin'!" said Gephart. "Him!"
>
> "What would Sam do," wondered Lefty, "if they played baseball with only one base? He wouldn't enjoy the game if he couldn't throw to the wrong one."
>
> "That play's liable to cost us somethin'," said Gephart.

Lardner's fictional world, however, is not restricted to the baseball diamond; its scope covers semi-literacy, insensitivity, stupidity, and pathos in many areas of American life. The dialogue between the talkative nurse and her patient in "Zone of Quiet" is typically revealing:

> "What's that you're reading?"
>
> " 'Vanity Fair,' " replied the man in bed.
>
> " 'Vanity Fair,' I thought that was a magazine."
>
> "Well, there's a magazine AND a book. This is the book."
>
> "Is it about a girl?"
>
> "Yes."
>
> "I haven't read it yet. I've been busy making this thing for my sister's birthday. She'll be twenty-nine. It's a bridge table cover."

A special object of satiric attack is the easy egotism of the 1920s that one can accomplish whatever one sets out to achieve. In Lardner's stories a semi-literate golf caddy can believe he can get the "nag" of writing newspaper articles. Jack Keefe believes unshakably that he is a better pitcher than Walter Johnson. The golden honeymooner believes in his mastery of checkers, horseshoes, and women. Two aspiring lyrics writers, Chas. F. Lewis and Harry Hart, believe they can write masterpieces. When these characters do fail, their shortcomings are outrageously rationalized away or just ignored. Jack Keefe never loses a game himself; it is always because of errors behind him, a sore arm, a bad climate, or stupid managerial strategy. Mabelle Gillespie of "Some Like Them Cold" cannot admit that she has been jilted; instead, she has a new "man friend" who forbids her further correspondence with Chas. F. Lewis. The golfers in "A Caddy's Diary" are obliged to cheat rather than admit that anyone else is a better player. Jim Kendall of "Haircut" camouflages his failures as husband and provider with cruel practical jokes which achieve for him the reputation of town practical joker. Mr. Shelton of "Contract" laments that all the bridge players he knows feel that they are authorities on the game and that "God sent them into the world to teach." Obviously there is an element of pathos in such blatant deception. Perhaps the most pathetic of Lardner's protagonists is Stephen Gale, the gas company bookkeeper of "The Maysville Minstrel," who, uniquely in Lardner's fictional world, realizes not only the intellectual emptiness which prohibits his success as a poet but that there is nothing he can do about it. Whether they realize it or not, Lardner's characters fail, as do most of Shakespeare's villains, because of a combination of ignorance and excessive ambition. Lardner has captured here something of the ethos of an age in which bellboys viewed themselves as stock market authorities and the ebullient parties of the Gatsbys were anticipated in perpetuity.

Those who persist in viewing Lardner as a sportswriter may be surprised to discover that his cynicism extends to athletics. It is wrong to say that the early "busher" stories ridicule the game; most of Lardner's early ballplayers are no worse than men of other occupations, but in 1921, after the Black Sox Scandal two years earlier, Lardner, judging sport by utilitarian principles, attacked the American custom of worshipping sports heroes, on the grounds that it generally resulted in the substitution of spectator sportsmanship for actual participation:

> Hero-worship is the national disease that does most to keep the grandstands full and the playgrounds empty. To hell with those four extra years of life which exercise might provide if they are going to cut in on our afternoon at the Polo Grounds, where, in blissful asininity, we may feast our eyes on the swarthy Champion of Swat, shouting now and then in an excess of anile idolatry, "Come on, you Babe. Come on, you Baby Doll!"

Such stories as "Champion," "A Frame-Up," or "A Caddy's Diary" reveal the athlete as frequently insensitive and dishonest. In "My Roomy" the ball-player is homicidally insane, and in both "Champion" and "Hurry Kane" the athlete actually accepts a bribe to throw a contest.

The mingling of this cynicism with the humor evident in Lardner's depiction of American life, though it does not reach the misanthropy of which Clifton Fadiman accused him, does help to explain the reluctance with which Lardner exposed his personal feelings. Of Lardner, Fitzgerald wrote: "He got some satisfaction from the reiterated statements of Mencken and F.P.A. as to his true stature as a writer. But I don't think he cared then—it is hard to understand but I don't think he really gave a damn about anything except his personal relations with people." Certainly Lardner had no faith in the collective intelligence of mankind—his view was probably the converse of the less admirable modern humanitarian view, in which one loves groups but exhibits indifference to (or even hates) individuals—but he never lacked close friends. His affection for Fitzgerald is well known, as was his camaraderie with such newspaper men as Walter Eckersall, Grantland Rice, John Wheeler, and Hugh Fullerton. Human kindness and sympathy were a kind of ethical ideal for Lardner, though they usually go unrewarded in his fictional world.

Perhaps Lardner's cynicism was also a factor in his lackadaisical response to Perkins's initial letter. In any case, *How to Write Short Stories* was contracted, and the professional relationship between Perkins and Lardner soon assumed social overtones. By 2 February 1924, Lardner was reminding Perkins of the eventful auto ride with Fitzgerald to Great Neck in July 1923, when Fitzgerald whimsically drove Perkins into Durand's pond "because it seemed more fun": "Why not visit Great Neck again? It's safer now, as Durand's pond is frozen over." On 9 May the Perkinses were invited to the Lardner home on Great Neck, with the host's comment that "dinner is at seven o'clock and I have outgrown my dinner clothes." Apparently the spirits of the era of bathtub gin prevailed, for Perkins later reported to Fitzgerald: "I meant to have a serious talk with him, but we arrived late and the drinks were already prepared. We did no business that night. He was very amusing." Immediately afterward the correspondence assumes a first-name basis and a markedly informal tone. It is interesting to observe that Lardner, after making the first overture, jumps back momentarily to "Dear Mr. Perkins" apparently before he has received Perkins's first "Dear Ring" response. Some time later, after the *Saturday Evening Post* had repeatedly requested Perkins to persuade Lardner to attend a luncheon, Perkins wrote casually to Lardner: "I really don't think it is a matter of any importance, but I promised to pass the invitation on to you. If you feel that it is too hot, don't come and I will make matters right." Lardner replied: "I'll come . . . if you think it advisable, but it is my secret ambition not to." When Perkins asked for a copy of the Bobbs-Merrill *Gullible's Travels,* so that the volume could be included in the set of Lardner's works which Scribner's published in 1925, Lardner answered: "I haven't a copy myself. Gene Buck has, and if you just want to read it, I'll try to get it away from him for a few days. It isn't that he is so fond of it, but they have got great big bookcases." The same letter concludes with an invitation to the Perkinses to visit the Lardner home again, where "I'd promise to be cold sober and nice, but not amusing." In March 1925, Perkins, after waiting six weeks for Lardner's promised prefaces to the Scribner's editions of *Gullible's Travels, You Know Me Al,* and *The Big Town,* expressed his anxiety. Lardner replies succinctly: "The principal cause of delay has been lack of an idea." On another occasion, Perkins is sufficiently moved by Lardner's "Haircut" to write: "I can't shake it out of my mind;-in fact the impression it made has deepened with time . . . But it is a most bitter and revealing story and I'd like to say so." Lardner's straightforward reply is one word: "Thanks."

Perkins is essentially the straight man in this correspondence, more business-like and less humorous than Lardner, but able fully to appreciate wit. In a mid-1925 letter, for example, he chuckles over complaints to the *New York Times* about a favorable article on Lardner by Henry Stuart: "The Times . . . received a number of indignant letters from old readers who said they could not understand such an article on a writer who did not even know GRAMMAR. I think they even went so far as to say you did not know how to spell. This is a grand world." But Perkins's contributions to Lardner's work were substantial. One value of this correspondence is the detail with which it demonstrates a famous editor at work with a talented if unenthusiastic author. Perkins did not have the literary tools of a Fitzgerald, a Hemingway, or a Lardner—"I am not under any illusions about myself as a humorist," he wrote—but he did have, as mentioned earlier, an uncanny ability both to recognize talent and, in a warmly human way, to obtain the most from that talent. An excerpt from a letter to Hemingway, a year after Lardner died, reveals how keenly Perkins perceived Lardner's potential:

> No one could have admired or been more fond of Ring than I was . . . . Ring was not, strictly speaking, a great writer. The truth is he never regarded himself seriously as a writer. He

always thought of himself as a newspaperman, anyhow. He had a sort of provincial scorn of literary people. If he had written much more, he would have been a great writer perhaps, but whatever it was that prevented him from writing more was the thing that prevented him from being a great writer. But he was a great man, and one of immense latent talent which got itself partly expressed.

Perkins made clear his "huge enjoyment" of Lardner's work from the beginning, and consistently reiterated his encouragement in the letters. Frequently it took the form of urging Lardner either to write more stories for next year's volume or, preferably, to "take a year off . . . and quietly do a novel": "I wish there were something I could do to compel you to write that 40,000 word story, or novel, or whatever it ought to be called. I do not know of any publishing news that would be more interesting than that such a book by you was to come out." It was also Perkins who suggested the burlesque introductions to stories in *How to Write Short Stories,* who had much to do with the specific grouping of Lardner's writing into books, who counseled, for instance, that in the light of the disappointing sales of Fitzgerald's *Gatsby,* which Perkins attributed to the brevity of the book, Lardner should delay the projected publication of *The Love Nest and Other Stories* until more stories could be added. Occasionally Perkins supplied chapter headings and even book titles: *The Love Nest and Other Stories* was his suggestion, as was *Round Up,* for the latter of which he has been criticized. But even though that title is misleading, it probably did enhance the sale of the volume, which was a Literary Guild selection and sold about 100,000 copies in the first year of publication.

In spite of Perkins's urging, Lardner never wrote the novel for which Perkins had asked. In the late 1920s, when he might have done it (regardless of some limitations in the handling of plot), his cynicism had grown to the point where he could not attribute sufficient importance to the writing of a longer fictional work. Also, he had become preoccupied with music and the theater. Music was something Lardner loved from his boyhood involvements with the Niles amateur theater group, and he delighted in experimenting with musical comedy. Many of his later stories are set in musical environments and deal with musicians: "Some Like Them Cold," "Rhythm," "A Day with Conrad Green," "Nora," etc. *June Moon,* his stage hit of 1929 (in collaboration with George S. Kaufman), was, though a non-musical, about the musical world and was his outstanding success in this vein. Lardner had no illusions about the musical scene, however, especially after his contacts with Florenz Ziegfeld. Writing about the Lyric Writers' Union, he once said: "Membership . . . is limited to boys and girls who graduated from school at the age of three." And Ziegfeld was the model for the thoroughly despicable Broadway producer of "A Day with Conrad Green."

Later, poor health, the result of heavy drinking in which Lardner had intermittently indulged from his early newspaper days, prevented sustained composition. While Perkins continued to press for more and longer works, Lardner grew more dejected: "My health hasn't been so good—I guess I am paying for my past—and I'm not averaging more than four short stories a year," he wrote early in 1931. In these last letters, the letterheads on the stationery poignantly reveal Lardner's quest for a cure, as he shifted about the country shortly before his death. In the fall of 1932, depressed over some rejections, he began to doubt his work: "Early in the summer," he wrote to Perkins, "one of the Post's associate editors wrote me such a tactless letter, suggesting that the new series of baseball letters be brought to a conclusion . . . that I, then in a low mental condition, thought the whole series must be pretty bad though I had felt quite proud of part of it when I had sent it in." Eight months before he died, he lamented to Perkins from his New York hospital bed: "Once I wrote a complete story, 'Alibi Ike,' between 2 P.M. and midnight, with an hour off for dinner. This last one was begun in July and finished ten days ago, and the Post turned it down just as promptly as it had accepted 'Ike'."

Lardner died of a heart attack on 25 September 1933. In the midst of a depression, with the publishing business suffering along with the rest of the country, Perkins had been able to do little except sympathize with his friend, and perhaps experience frustration at the knowledge that Lardner would never write his novel. This correspondence strongly implies, however, that Perkins probably succeeded in obtaining far more fiction from Lardner than anyone else would have been likely to do.

THE CORRESPONDENCE OF RING LARDNER AND MAXWELL PERKINS

F. Scott Fitzgerald had an eye for talent and a passion to see it recognized in his friends. His role in bringing Hemingway to Scribner's is literary history, but the result of his success in persuading Maxwell Perkins to read Ring Lardner's uncollected stories early in 1923 is even more curious—made so by Lardner's distinct lack of enthusiasm at the prospect of being transformed into a literary man. Unlike Fitzgerald or Hemingway, Lardner felt little need to earn money from the assemblage of his stories into books, nor did he apparently yearn for recognition from the intelligentsia as a serious writer. Prior to the publication of *How To Write Short Stories* in 1924, literary critics had not generally identified Lardner as anything more than a newspaper humorist and a philologist of some note. Nevertheless, in 1923 Lardner was, chiefly as a result of his widely syndicated weekly newspaper column, among the ten best-known men in America, earning over $30,000 a year and enjoying the adulation of his fellow journalists and a large popular audience who viewed him as a great wit that had never "gone literary." Such acclaim necessitated the tact with which Perkins approaches Lardner in the opening letter. The correspondence that follows is the record of a highly personable and persuasive editor skillfully cajoling an amazingly reluctant author into cooperating in the collection of a substantial amount of memorable fiction.

JULY 2, 1923

Dear Mr. Lardner:

I read your story "The Golden Wedding" with huge enjoyment. Scott Fitzgerald recommended it to me and he also suggested that you might have other material of the same sort, which, with this, could form a volume. I am therefore writing to tell you how very much interested we should be to consider this possibility, if you could put the material before us. I would hardly have ventured to do this if Scott had not spoken of the possibility, because your position in the literary world is such that you must be besieged by publishers, and to people in that situation their letters of interest are rather a nuisance. I am certainly mighty glad to have the chance of expressing our interest though, if, as Scott thought, you would not feel that we were merely bothering you. Would you be willing to send on any material that might go with "The Golden Wedding" to form a volume, or to tell me where I might come at it in periodicals?

Very truly yours,

Originally published in the July 1922 *Cosmopolitan,* "The Golden Honeymoon," to which Perkins is referring, has always been one of Lardner's most popular short stories. Critical assessments of it have, however, varied considerably. At one extreme, Donald Elder has described the honeymooners as "rather amiable bores." On the other hand, Clifton Fadiman has called the piece "one of the most smashing indictments of a 'happy marriage' ever written." In fact the narrative, one of Lardner's subtlest, does exhibit tolerance for these "bores," but when one views the story as a whole, the pettiness of the characters' lives is unmistakable, and the indictment is there, though Fadiman overstates his case.

It is interesting to note the gap of five months between Perkins's offer and Lardner's first extant response, below. However, an agreement must have been reached by 19 September 1923, by which time Perkins was requesting back copies of the *Saturday Evening Post* and other magazines in which Lardner's stories had appeared. Astonishingly, Lardner had not bothered to keep copies of his own stories!

GREAT NECK, NEW YORK
DECEMBER FIFTH.

Dear Mr. Perkins:-

I enclose a (and, I guess, the only) copy of "Champion", which Scott tells me you have been looking for. I'm sorry to have kept you waiting.

Sincerely,

First published in the October 1916 *Metropolitan* magazine, "Champion" remains one of Lardner's most controversial stories, though not artistically one of his best. Fadiman called it "a brutal masterpiece" and Gilbert Seldes wrote that it "makes you quiver with a rage which the author himself dispassionately seems not to share." In contrast, James Frakes labels the story "heavy melodrama—a country where he is not at home." Frakes is right. "Champion" is a scathing denunciation of newspaper glorification of the sports hero, but, as Heywood Campbell Broun wrote, "The sawed-off shotgun shows too visibly above the rushes."

DEC. 7, 1923

Dear Mr. Lardner:

Thanks for the copy of "The Champion". I am mighty glad to get it at last. I had tried advertising and everything else;- but I did find in the end that there was one other copy, H. L. Mencken's.

Now I have all the stories you spoke of that eventful night when Scott drove into the lake. What an excellent sport he is about the failure of "The Vegetable"!

Sincerely yours,

It is hardly surprising that Perkins should have contemplated borrowing a copy of "Champion" from H. L. Mencken. Mencken, who was then literary editor of the *Smart Set,* and who was to found the *American Mercury* in 1924, was one of the first to bestow serious literary acclaim on Lardner, praising him in *The American Language* primarily for Lardner's excellent rendering of American dialogue.

The references in the above letter to Fitzgerald have to do with his auto driving and with his play. A favorite eating and drinking place on Long Island was René Durand's restaurant at Manhasset, where on one occasion Perkins, Lardner, and Fitzgerald apparently discussed the make-up of Lardner's projected volume of short stories, and where Fitzgerald imbibed too freely and drove Perkins into a nearby pond when the two attempted to leave. The incident occurred in July 1923, and a year later Perkins recalled the experience in a letter to Fitzgerald: "I had yesterday a disillusioning afternoon at Great Neck, not in respect to Ring Lardner, who gains on you whenever you see him, but in respect to Durant's where he took me for lunch. I thought that night a year ago that we ran down a steep place into a lake. There was no steep place and no lake. We sat on a balcony in front. It was dripping hot and Durant took his police dog down to the margin of that puddle of a lily pond,- the dog waded almost across it;- and I'd been calling it a lake all these months. But they've put up a fence to keep others from doing as we did." *The Vegetable* was Fitzgerald's attempt at a three-act comedy. Though he worked on it for over a year, it played for only a week before closing in November 1923 at the Apollo Theater in Atlantic City.

Dear Mr. Lardner:

I thought your preface was excellent and I showed it to two or three others here who enjoyed it immensely. If only I could get those three stories out of the Post we would be in a position to take up the question immediately and finally. I have followed my first letter asking for the numbers with quite an emotional appeal. It may accomplish something.

Sincerely yours,

P.S. Hovey[1] has had "The Facts" copied and is sending it so the three Post stories are the only ones needed at present.

Perkins refers above to the burlesque preface to *How To Write Short Stories,* on the "technic" of writing the short story. Those who contend that Lardner did not value his work highly will note that Lardner did not bother to write a new preface; he simply revised an old newspaper column. Although *Printer's Ink* thought the preface a "complimentary" device which distinguished the book from other short story collections, most critics took a contrary view. Edmund Wilson, for example, wrote: "The nonsense preface is so far below his usual humorous level that one suspects him of a guilty conscience at attempting to disguise an excellent piece of literature as a Stephen Leacock buffoonery." In

1. Carl Hovey, editor of METROPOLITAN magazine.

any case, the preface served to remind Lardner's large following of relatively unintellectual readers that he was still their unspoiled newspaper humorist. Here is a typical passage from the preface:

> How to begin—or, as we professionals would say, "how to commence"—is the next question. It must be admitted that the method of approach ("L'approchement") differs even among first class fictionists. For example, Blasco Ibanez usually starts his stories with a Spanish word, Jack Dempsey with an "I" and Charley Peterson with a couple of simple declarative sentences about his leading character, such as "Hazel Gooftree had just gone mah jong. She felt faint."

MIAMI BEACH FLO JAN 25 1924
MAXWELL E PERKINS
    CARE CHARLES SCRIBNERS SONS 597 FIFTH
AVE NEWYORKNY
PLEASE SEND NEXT PROOFS TO NEW COLONIAL
HOTEL NASSAU BAHAMAS
RING LARDNER

Fᴇʙ. 1, 1924

Dear Mr. Lardner:

I hope Scott has told you that we have actually gone so far as to put your "How To Write Short Stories" into the spring list;- a rather irregular proceeding since you have never told us we could. But we were very much interested in the general idea and we felt that the best thing to do was to act immediately and get out a volume. If this seems right to you, we will pay a fifteen percent royalty from the start on this first book.

I am having a bad time getting together the stories though. I have a letter from McClure's saying that they haven't got the issue for August 1915, and the Post did not have any story in the issue of December 6, 1919. I sent Scott a list of the stories that the Cosmopolitan had and will copy for us. I can have the Post looked through in the library between 1914 and 1919 — for after that the Post is indexed — and see what we find and I think we can arrange to have the stories copied out. We will do the same with McClure's for August 1915. If we get these stories we will have a good representative collection.

Sincerely yours,

The three *Saturday Evening Post* stories which Perkins had difficulty obtaining copies of were "Horseshoes," "Some Like Them Cold," and "A Caddy's Diary." Most of Lardner's early stories were published in the *Post*.

The story published by *Mc-Clure's* magazine was "Harmony," an unpretentious early story distinguished chiefly by its beautifully realistic dialogue of the baseball dugout. Perkins was somewhat misled by the titles of the *Cosmopolitan* pieces, for actually Lardner published only one story, "The Golden Honeymoon," in *Cosmopolitan* prior to 1925, along with a number of non-fiction pieces. These and the other short stories for which Perkins was searching were finally obtained by photostating back copies of magazines in the New York City Public Library.

GREAT NECK, NEW YORK
FEBRUARY SECOND.

Dear Mr. Perkins:-

The arrangement and terms are satisfactory to me. I'm sorry you have had so much trouble gathering the stuff.

Why not visit Great Neck again? It's safer now, as Durand's pond is frozen over.

Sincerely,

FEB. 18, 1924

Dear Mr. Lardner:

Although I am notified by the Post that "Horseshoes" is on the way, I am not waiting for it, but am putting all the other stories in hand, in the following order:

> How to Write Short Stories
> The Facts
> Some Like 'Em Cold
> Alibi Ike
> Golden Honeymoon
> Champion
> My Roomy
> A Caddy's Diary
> A Frame-Up
> Harmony

You may not like this order, but it can easily be changed in the galleys. I considered first more or less grouping the stories but gave up the idea and went in the other direction;– that is, I aimed at variety. I thought that the several baseball stories ought to be scattered through the volume, for instance. The question of the first story was a hard one, but it could not be "The Golden Honeymoon" because that had appeared in the "Short Stories of 1922" volume. I did not think it ought to be a baseball story anyhow, because we want to place the emphasis differently in this whole scheme. I finally hit upon "The Facts" because it will please everybody, male and female, of every sort. Then I followed with "Some Like 'em Cold" because it seemed to me to be a masterpiece in that sort of writing. At this point it seemed well to get in one of the baseball stories and "Alibi Ike" is a corker. I am sorry "Champion" comes so late in a way, but publishers probably exaggerate the importance of an early position. People don't begin at the beginning and read a book of stories straight through. The stories that follow I have arranged on the principle of variety.

I have been very anxious to get this book into the actual process of manufacture, but as soon as the proofs begin to come up, I will try to get you to let me take up with you the question of the earlier books, and the plan of gathering them in from the publishers.

Sincerely yours,

P.S. That chauffeur that drove us from Scott's to your house was greatly excited to know that he had been driving Ring Lardner.

Perkins's selection of "The Facts" as the opening story in the volume is a curious one, since it is probably the least of the stories in the book. It is simply a magazine narrative, with a highly contrived, trite plot, concerning an engagement broken off at Christmas because the prospective groom gets drunk with a friend and sends inappropriate gifts to the members of his fiancée's prudish household. Max Eastman, however, called it Lardner's "most humorous story"!

The other stories Perkins stresses above are among Lardner's best. With the exception of "Haircut," "Some Like Them Cold" is probably Lardner's most anthologized story. It is a satire on the institutionalized American romance, achieved through the epistolary genre Lardner had used so successfully in *You Know Me Al.* His mastery of the form here is illustrated by the fact that he is able to lay *two* personalities bare through their mutual correspondence. The story reveals both the pitiful overtures of Mabelle Gillespie to catch a man before she becomes old and the shallow replies of the ignorant know-it-all provincial, Charles F. Lewis, who has come to the Big Town to write song hits. Elizabeth Bibesco calls it one of those stories which "belong to the universal masterpieces that know no frontiers." "Alibi Ike" as a literary work does not compare with Lardner's best stories—it is a somewhat overly long catalogue of baseball player Frank X. Farrell's excuses to his teammates for whatever he does, good or bad—but it was so successful that the title has become a catch word in our language (Hollywood made an early movie of it, with Joe E. Brown playing Ike).

MARCH 17, 1924

Dear Mr. Lardner:

I have sent you some of the galley proof and will follow rapidly with the rest. Will you read it quickly?

We have had trouble with the wrap and called in Scott for consultation. Held* fell down on the case, at least we thought so. But everything is going well now, I think. On the side of the cover we are going to reproduce your signature.

Now here is an idea. Reject it if you want to, of course, but do give it thought. We have always felt there was a little

* John Held Jr., famous for his LIFE "Flapper" caricatures.

weakness in the title, that the intent of it was not strongly enough expressed in the book. It occurred to me that you might write a comment on each story, suiting the comment of course, to each story so that its quality would accordingly vary, but which would carry on the general spirit and idea of the preface. This comment might in some cases be only a couple of lines long and in none more than twenty lines. We would then precede each story with a half title page — a page normally blank except for the title. Under this title, probably in italics, would be printed this comment on the story which would represent each one, amusing and satirical as an illustration of short story writing. Maybe your idea of it would be different even if you did make the comment, but if you made it according to your idea I know it would add immensely to the interest of the book and would help immensely in the whole matter of publicity, etc. Please consider it.

My remembrances to Mrs. Lardner. I hope you are having a good time.

Sincerely,

Dear Mr. Lardner:

I hope the proof is getting to you safely,- rather a superfluous observation since if it does not, this letter won't. We ought now to consider the question of getting the other books released by their publishers, Bobbs Merrill and Doran. It would be much better strategy if you approached them. Could you write them saying that since the books were no longer active (assuming that they are not) you would like to get control of them, and asking what the steps would be thereto? This would let us know where we stand and when we heard from them we could say whether we thought the suggestion they made was fair. I am going on the assumption that we would be responsible for whatever the expense was, of course. We ought to get this matter well under way before the book is out, and we want to get it out as rapidly as we can.

Sincerely yours,

Lardner's compliance with Perkins's request to write Bobbs-Merrill and Doran evoked an agonized response from his friend Hewitt H. Howland, editor at Bobbs-Merrill:

The Bobbs Merrill Company
Publishers — Indianapolis
April 19, 1924

Dear Ring:
Your letter sent me to the hospital for repairs; hence the delay in replying. I am still running a temperature, clear up over the transom, as Riley used to say, and am dictating this letter while the doctor and the nurse have their backs turned—not on each other.
As Brown says when Smith dies: Why, I can't believe it. I saw him only three days ago and he never looked better. If you were going to some—but are you really going? And why do

you have to "stick with 'em" as you say, just because they happened to have an idea? This getting an author with the uniform edition bait is such an old wheeze. Listen—if I lose you I'll probably lose my job, and it's a long time since I worked. I'd starve and you'd have me on your conscience and be most uncomfortable.

You ask if we'd set a price on the plates of your books. As for me, I'd as soon sell my fee simple in my brother-in-law. But Lawrence Chambers will be in New York next week. Get hold of him, and there may be another story, as the girl said to the soldier.

The doctor and the nurse have come to and are saying that if there is any dictating to be done they'll do it. And if you could see the nurse!

Yours,
H.H.H.

No record of Doran's response survives, but agreements were reached by October 1924.

THE NEW WILLARD, WASHINGTON.
MARCH TWENTY-SECOND.

Dear Mr. Perkins:-

I think the preface idea is a good one. I'll try to carry it out if it isn't too late. How soon would I have to come through?

The proofs are here, but I haven't had time to go over them yet. I will be here till next Friday or Saturday.

Sincerely,

In addition to the burlesque general preface, Lardner, following Perkins's suggestion, wrote brief comparable commentaries to accompany each story. For example, "Champion" is described as "an example of the mystery story. The mystery is how it came to get printed." "The Golden Honeymoon" is summarized as "a story with 'sex appeal.' " Like the general preface, these "introductions" were not very well received by the critics, who mostly interpreted them as ridicule of conventional composition manuals, and thus as a lampoon upon the literary world which had previously ignored Lardner's work. It has been suggested by several, and first by Fitzgerald, in his eulogy of Lardner, that Lardner perhaps came to regard himself as a half-educated writer and that through such prefaces and his mock autobiography later he was bitterly satirizing his own efforts. It appears true that Lardner's satiric strain progressively deepens, but it is difficult to hold the view that Lardner's fictional world was limited to the dimensions of the ballpark, or that he regarded his knowledge as shallow. After his very early stories, based on his experiences as a reporter traveling with the Cubs and White Sox, Lardner wrote about many aspects of the vast American middle class—the lyrics writers, bridge players, producers, barbers, bellboys, policemen, nurses, and gas company workers that he knew from his midwestern childhood and his later urban New York environment. To attribute the limitations of these fictional characters to Lardner himself is to ignore the probable purpose of his satire; Lardner sympathized with these people, but the guise that he was one of them was merely that. Lardner was well-read and better educated than most.

MARCH 24, 1924

Dear Mr. Lardner:

Time *is* valuable, but I think what you might add on the line discussed is more valuable. Anyway, we will save time by not sending you any page proof: we will have it read here and will make sure that all your changes are followed. The best course would be for you to do each of the comments as you read the galleys and then to return the galleys progressively with the comments. Then we could go into pages as the galleys came back and even cast the pages perhaps, before all the galleys were back.

As your letter comes from Washington, I suppose you are busy at something. I had pictured you as chiefly occupied with golf, or Mah Jongg, from what Scott said. I supposed you were at Southern Pines[2] or somewhere like that.

Sincerely yours,

GREAT NECK, NEW YORK
WEDNESDAY.

Dear Mr. Perkins:

I enclose prefaces for Harmony and Horseshoes. The proofs and copy are going under separate covers.

Sincerely,

THE NEW WILLARD,
WASHINGTON.
MARCH 27.

Dear Mr. Perkins:-

I will try to show up in your office on Monday with all the galleys and everything. I think that would be the simplest way of getting things finished up. I will call you Monday forenoon. And that's the last sentence I intend to start with an I till my next letter.

Sincerely,

2. Lardner occasionally played golf at the Pine Needles Country Club in Southern Pines, North Carolina.

APRIL 1, 1924

Dear Mr. Lardner:

If you had come in today instead of yesterday, I could have shown you the wrap. I just saw a final proof, and it is really excellent. One thing I should have asked you for,- your picture. We want it in order to make a drawing from it to use in advertising.

Hoping your visit to the capital is now only a pleasant memory, I am,

Yours,

Perkins's request probably re-
sulted in the sketch by Ellen Graham
Anderson now in the University of
Virginia Library.

MAY 8, 1924

Dear Mr. Lardner:

I am sending you now six copies of "How to Write Short Stories". I meant to bring them to you personally and then to talk over what might be the next move but I have a deuce of a cold and do not want to give it to anyone else. If I should come down some day next week would I be likely to find you? I don't think that either Bobbs Merrill or Doran would be at all likely to do what we aim to do and I think they would be willing to help us in doing it,- that is, to publish a uniform set of say five volumes, on some basis that would be practicable. We have often done this and never had much difficulty in it. What has troubled me more is the matter of formulating the set, for Scott's scheme made up over the lunch table does not seem to work out very well. I .would like to talk to you about this for a few minutes, and also about what you will do later.

Everybody here is delighted with these stories. We have distributed them widely to individuals and I would like to send out a lot of others to individuals you might suggest for some personal reason. This too, we could take up.

Then there was the matter of the photograph. We ought to have one. What we want to do is to present you after the manner of the blurb on the back of the wrap and we should be very much helped in this with your pictures.

Sincerely yours,

No record of Fitzgerald's plan survives, but the decision finally arrived at was to reissue, under Scribner's label, *Ẏou Know Me Al, Gullible's Travels,* and *The Big Town* in 1925.

Dear Mr. Perkins:-

Sorry you have a cold. We never have them in Great Neck.

I will be home all day every day next week excepting Monday. My wife says (and we speak as one), can you and Mrs. Perkins come to dinner Tuesday night (or Wednesday, Thursday, Friday or Saturday night)? The telephone is Great Neck 103. If you drive out and can't find the place, call up from the drug store and we'll come and pilot you. Dinner is at seven o'clock and I have outgrown my dinner clothes. If you accept this invitation I will give you my photograph.

Sincerely,

MAY 10, 1924

Dear Mr. Lardner:

We'll be there at seven o'clock on Wednesday, and not in evening clothes. Thanks very much. Maybe I'll bring a carload of books to be autographed.

Sincerely,

Though not much was achieved professionally on this occasion, it was a great social success. Immediately after the dinner, the correspondence assumes a first-name basis.

Dear Mr. Perkins (or Max):-

I suppose you saw Burton Rascoe's[3] little piece.
Here are some more names:
Percy Hammond, 17 West 10th. Street, New York.
Alexander Woollcott, the City Club, New York.
Quinn Martin, Great Neck, N.Y.
Harvey T. Woodruff, c/o Chicago Tribune, Chicago,
Illinois.
W. O. McGeehan, New York Herald and Tribune.

Sincerely,

P.S. Next time you come out here, which I hope will be
soon, I will be different.
P.S.S. Also - adding to names - Herbert B. Swope,
New York World.

MAY 24, 1924

Dear Ring:

I suppose you would see the enclosed[4] anyway, but it is
good so I thought I would send it in case it might not come
to you otherwise.
You saw that Kenelm Digby headed his column with

---

3. Burton Rascoe, literary editor of the CHICAGO TRIBUNE (1912-20) while
Lardner was writing his "In the Wake of the News" column (1913-19) for
the same newspaper. Rascoe wrote a syndicated column, "The Daybook of a
New Yorker" from 1924 through 1928. In 1927 he became editor of BOOK-
MAN. In later years he was mostly a free-lance writer.
4. Probably one of a number of favorable reviews of HOW TO WRITE SHORT
STORIES.

the book last week. I have sent it to those additional people you named in the list you sent. Next week in the Times we are going to have a truly effective ad. I wish you could come up here sometime and meet some of the people and stay for lunch. Mr. Scribner, who came back only recently from California, is very much impressed with your stories and I want to have him meet you.

Scott has an excellent story[5]— as good writing as he has ever done — in the new Mercury.

We enjoyed being at your house very much. Please thank Mrs. Lardner for being so good to us.

Yours,

GREAT NECK, NEW YORK
MAY 27TH.

Dear Mr. Perkins:-

I enclose what I have nicknamed the perfect blurb. Thanks for sending me the Post's.

I also enjoyed Scott's "Absolution" though some of it was over my partly bald head.

Mencken writes that he is reviewing my book at length in the July Mercury.

Did I put James J. Montague on that list? I meant to. His address is c/o The Bell Syndicate, 154 Nassau Street, New York City. And another one is Hugh S. Fullerton, c/o Liberty, 25 Park Place, New York City. I hope I haven't overdrawn my account, but anyway I promise this is the finish.

Sincerely, ·

5. "Absolution," in the June 1924 AMERICAN MERCURY.

The clipping Lardner enclosed, from the *Boston Transcript*, advertises *How To Write Short Stories* thus: "Ten short stories by an American humorist, with a brief prefatory explanation of methods of writing them."

The Mencken review appeared in the June 1924 *American Mercury*. After lamenting the failure of professors to recognize Lardner's talent, Mencken assessed that talent thus:

> His studies, to be sure, are never very profound; he makes no attempt to get at the primary springs of passion and motive; all his people share the same amiable stupidity, the same transparent vanity, the same shallow inconsequentiality; they are all human Fords, and absolutely alike at bottom. But if he thus confines himself to the surface, it yet remains a fact that his investigations on that surface are extraordinarily alert, ingenious and brilliant—that the character he finally sets before us, however roughly articulated as to bones, is so astoundingly realistic as to hide that the effect is indistinguishable from that of life itself. The old man in "The Golden Honeymoon" is not merely well done; he is perfect. And so is the girl in "Some Like Them Cold." And so, even, is the idiotic Frank X. Farrell in "Alibi Ike"—an extravagant grotesque and yet quite real from glabella to calcaneus.

Lardner's pretense at not understanding Fitzgerald's "Absolution"
perhaps stems from his reaction to sexual overtones in Fitzgerald's story,
which deals with the sexual frustra-
tions of a priest. Lardner uses the expression "over my head" often as the
ultimate dismissal. It does not appear
always to indicate prudery but may
simply reflect the contra-intellectuality
of a thoughtful, brooding, inner-di-
rected man for whom both the world
of the flesh and the world of the mind
had fairly prescriptive limits.

MAY 29, 1924

Dear Ring:

I thought the enclosed would amuse you. It is a voice
from early Victorian time, almost. The author must be well
over eighty. We have been publishing for her for generations,
and she has done some good writing. She desired to see your
book because she noticed that it was the only other book of
short stories on our list. So I sent it with great curiosity as to
what she would make of it; for in addition to being English
and old, she is sort of a grande dame.

There was a letter in Broun's column[6] about the book
and you will have seen reviews in the World and Times,- the
Times very unsatisfactory, and I thought stupid. Does the
author think that Homer wrote the Iliad with the intention of
showing the character of the civilization of that time?

Sincerely,

6. "It Seems to Me," in the NEW YORK WORLD.

The *New York World* review (25 May 1924), by "A. K.," had strong praise for *How To Write Short Stories:* "There is not another writer of English who could do this book. There is not another with the humor, the skill, the penetration or the lowly touch. There are better books and better writers, but Mr. Lardner is the only one who could have accomplished this particular feat, and it is all joyous reading." The *New York Times* review (25 May 1924), by J. Donald Adams, expressed a desire to see "more range" in Lardner's work. Adams admitted that Lardner's use of vernacular was excellent but suggested that Lardner did not plumb the depths of contemporary human nature as he might.

Unfortunately, "the enclosed" does not survive, but another interesting response to the book, written probably by Jasper Barnett Cowdin, an elderly minor poet, does:

To W. Ring Lardner

Drear Mr. Gardner: Wile you are out there on Long I. ware nobody can see you with your arms around Great Neck you are a cute one to twist your name around from Wedding Ring to Ring W. to keep out of scandal an I honor you for it. Now what I want is to learn how to write short stories that will sell for 2 dollars like yourn to bunk the public an still keep us respectable.

Years ago when the Black Cat was a household pet magazine that most famous authors couldnt get into I sold it a story of 19 hundred words for 35 bucks whereas at the same time Jack London sold his first one there 5 thousan words an got only 5 antelopes mourn I did. But he got the best of me later on for he sailed around the world in his own liner bought with his excess profits wile I perforce discreetly remained ashore.

Now Mr. Lardner I send 2 iron automatons and 9 stamps overplus for your new book hoping you will write in it a word or two of real affection fore me an sign your genuine name. If you have a 2d hand copy with your finger prints on the leaves Ill send extra stamps to cover enhanced value. In your letter to Gilbert Seldes you say you done it for nothing for some gal in Detroit an I was born there myself on Fort Street so why make distinction? I dont care for no costive Japanese badaeker as the folks in Woodhaven dont know its valubility but if the 9 stamps aint enough an you hold out for more I will send you a pome of mine satyrizing our funny american institution The Evolution of a President After

you have read it you will
sneak your own hat out of
the ring mighty prompt.
Brant Whitlock reformed
mare of Toledo an coun-
selor to Belgum wrote me
saying it nearly tickled him
to death I hope it will do
mourn that for you
    Expectantly yours
    J. B. Cowdin esq
10409 107th Avenue
Woodhaven, Long Island
N.Y.
    All other Cowdin's in
    N.Y. are millionairs
    but I am distingt

JUNE 11, 1924

Dear Ring:

I am enclosing some ads which perhaps you have seen,
one from the Post, one from the Times, and one from Scribner's. But chiefly I am writing to warn you to avoid 42nd
Street opposite 4th Avenue for the next several days (though
I imagine you are safely in Chicago, anyway) because you
are likely to be recognized there on account of the fact that
Liggetts have a large window display of "How To Write
Short Stories", an enormous enlargement of your picture,
and some pages of the preface. Printer's Ink had an article
which was highly complimentary to the device of the title and
preface, and comments on the stories as being a new way of
putting out a product so as to distinguish it.
    I wish you could manage to stop in here some time

because I want to have Mr. Scribner meet you. He is very
keen about the stories. He sent a copy to Barrie and I have
sent one to Galsworthy.

Yours,

John Galsworthy—author of *The
Forsyte Saga* and numerous other novels, plays, and essays—and Sir James
Barrie, the Scottish author notably of
The Little Minister and *Peter Pan,*
were among Scribner's coterie of famous authors in the 1920s. Donald
Elder asserts that Barrie's enthusiasm
for Lardner's work was a decisive factor in Scribner's decision to publish
Lardner's fiction. Barrie's introduction
to *The Young Visitors,* a novel supposedly by the twelve-year-old Daisy Ash-
ford, had also resulted in a Lardner
publication some years earlier. *The
Young Immigrunts,* published in 1920,
purports to be the narrative of Lardner's four-year-old son, Ring, Jr., of a
family auto trip from Goshen, Indiana,
to Greenwich, Connecticut, but is primarily a hilarious parody of the style
of the precocious author of *The Young
Visitors.* And Ring, Jr's "book" contains "a preface by the Father."

Dear Ring:

We have sold not far from 3500 copies of the book. Well, that is a small number actually, but it has not been out long and it has shown steady signs of increase. There is no use prophesying about such matters but if you had enough stories to make another collection we would be anxious to make a book of them for publication in the next season. I know you haven't enough, but I hope you will have before so very long. Do you think there is a chance of it? I know the next book would sell even better than this, and this one would certainly not stop selling after the first season, but would grow in sales. The only book of yours I haven't got now is "Gullible's Travels". I have been advertising for it without success. Haven't you a copy?

Sincerely yours,

Dear Ring:

I bet you decided to cover that convention from Great Neck. I am enclosing herewith a quotation from J. M. Barrie's letter to Mr. Scribner, giving another English view of your book. I begin to think better of the British.

Yours,

JULY 7, 1924

Dear Ring:

Wagstaff of the Post has been after me again to persuade you to come to lunch at the National Arts Club,–this
time on Wednesday, the day after tomorrow. Oliver Herford[7]
is one of the others who will be there and nobody will be
expected to make a speech or anything of that sort. The fact
is, the Post literary section is trying to keep on the map. I
really don't think it is a matter of any importance, but I
promised to pass the invitation on to you. If you feel that it is
too hot, don't come and I will make matters right. Could you
call me up to tomorrow a.m. and let me know?

Yours,

In the following letter Lardner's
frustration with the politics of the 1924
Democratic National Convention (it
lasted through 103 ballots), which he
covered as a reporter, is evident. In the
presidential election of 1924, John W.
Davis ran seven million votes behind
Calvin Coolidge, though he finished
three million votes ahead of the Pro-
gressive party's Robert M. LaFollette.
Lardner's dissatisfaction with the
Democrats is probably due to the various disputes that year among labor
groups within the party which led (after the convention) to a break between
the moderates who nominated Davis
and the more radical wing which preferred LaFollette. The failure of the

7. English-born poet and playwright, who wrote many books, most of which
he illustrated himself. Among his publications were A CHILD'S PRIMER OF
NATURAL HISTORY (1899) and THE DEB'S DICTIONARY (1931).

Democrats to resolve differences in-
sured their defeat and Coolidge's vic-
tory at the polls. Lardner generally
maintained a healthy cynicism towards
politics, though he did, at the request
of Heywood Broun, support Socialist
candidate Norman Thomas in the
1932 election. More interesting, however, is Lardner's reluctance in this
passage and elsewhere to use profane
language. In 1932 he angered many
popular lyricists and performers by
conducting from his hospital bed a
crusade in his *New Yorker* "Over the
Waves" column against popular songs
he considered suggestive or immoral.
In a 1934 *Esquire* piece Hemingway
asserted that this reluctance was Lardner's only flaw as a master of realistic
dialogue.

Dear Max:-

I do hope you will overlook or forgive or something my
rudeness in not replying sooner to your letters or telephone
calls—my alibi is the Democrats, God   them.

Now then (1) I am trying to get up nerve enough to ask
for release from the "comic" strip, which is me bete noir as
the Scotch have it; if I do that I will have a lot more time to
spend on short stories. (2). I'll come to one of those literary
luncheons if you think it advisable,but it is my secret ambition not to. (3). I enclose a letter from Mr. Darrow[8] which I
ought to have answered. Will you please tell him that I had a

8. Whitney Darrow was in charge of sales and promotion at Scribner's in
1924.

letter from Mr. Beach,[9] in which he not only repeated the request that I write something for his Book Notes, but also he wrote it himself as he thought I ought to write it and I wished you could see it; he put every gag into it except Alabama casts 24 votes for Underwood.[10] If Mr. Darrow thinks I'd better write something for them, I'll do it, but between you and me I have nicknamed the editor the Beach Nut. (4). I very much appreciate the way you are pushing the book. (5). I have virtually gone down on my knees to the Bobbs-Merrill people for a copy of Gullible's Travels, vainly. I haven't a copy myself. Gene Buck has, and if you just want to read it, I'll try to get it away from him for a few days. It isn't that he is so fond of it, but they have got great big bookcases.

I wish you would call up and get into a confidential conversation with me, the gist of which would be that we'd make an engagement for you and Mrs. Perkins to come to Great Neck and I'd promise to be cold sober and nice, but not amusing.

Sincerely,

From September 1922 to the fall of 1924 Lardner wrote a comic strip for the Bell Syndicate called "You Know Me, Al" based on the character of Jack Keefe, the protagonist of Lardner's popular book by that title. The illustrations were done by Dick Dorgan, the brother of the well-known

9. Probably Harrison L. Beach, a newspaperman.
10. During the 1924 Democratic National Convention, which, after a lengthy struggle between William McAdoo and Alfred Smith, nominated John Davis on the 103rd ballot, Alabama continually cast its 24 votes for its own Senator Oscar W. Underwood, in hopes of promoting him as a compromise candidate.

newspaper cartoonist Tad Dorgan, who was a good friend of Lardner. The strip appeared in over a hundred newspapers and brought Lardner about $20,000 a year, but then he became bored with the work and turned it over completely to Dick Dorgan, who continued it until May 1926.

Gene Buck, who owned a most likely unread copy of *Gullible's Travels,* was a songwriter and producer for Florenz Ziegfeld's Follies and a neighbor of Lardner in Great Neck. Lardner was occasionally amused by Buck's professional brainstorms and by his rather pretentious lifestyle. Lardner acknowledged that his short story "The Love Nest" was actually based on the Buck household. The story is a portrait of a marriage happy on the surface but in reality blighted by the husband's possessiveness, which causes his wife's sense of unfilfillment and her subsequent dipsomania.

The following letter was written after the Fitzgeralds had abandoned the social high life of Great Neck for France in the spring of 1924. Lardner, who had been left in charge of renting their house and taking care of assorted expenses, conscientiously restored order to Fitzgerald's chaotic financial arrangements and even covered Fitzgerald's Great Neck bank account later that year when Fitzgerald overdrew. Such action indicates again the close relationship between Fitzgerald and Lardner, at least during the year and a half when they were neighbors.

Dear Ring:

I have a letter this morning from Scott which begins with the question: "Is Ring dead?" I am sending him several of your syndicate articles which I got from the Bell Syndicate, which will prove you are not. He asks if his house is rented. I think you told me it was even as long ago as I was down in Great Neck. I have asked Mr. Snevily if he could send me the old Syndicate articles for I am sure we could make up a book from some of your material for after next January, and then there would be two volumes published by us and "Gullible's Travels," "The Big Town," and "You Know Me Al",- five volumes, which would be enough for the set. Couldn't you either see me sometime in New York or tell me some time when I could see you in Great Neck,- but not in the evening there, because we are living for the summer way up near New Canaan, in the country, and I ought to get home every night if possible.

I told Mrs. Lardner over the telephone that we had printed a fourth three thousand. We are, of course, running beyond the sales in the numbers printed but all goes well.

Yours,

July 31, 1924

Dear Ring:

I am enclosing herewith an early proof of an advertisement which will appear in the Times. It is the biggest we have put out on the book. The blank spaces you will infer are to be filled in with pictures, the idea being, of course, that readers will more easily notice the ad and will be curious to see what these gentlemen look like and will thereby give the whole matter more attention and be left with a distinct impression. I am sure it will be made a much more effective ad than it looks like without the pictures. Forgive us for speaking of you in the leading paragraph — in the interests of effect — as if your recognition as what the paragraph says you are recognized as being, were something new. Of course it is not among those who are conversant with writing, but it makes an effective lead-off to put it that way.

I find myself all tied up because in this supposedly dull season, when all the New York authors go away, Kansas, Paris and Chappaqua authors come on to see New York,- and their publishers. But I am going to call up Monday to ask you if I could come down on either Tuesday or Wednesday, and I will come out any time on either of those days that is convenient. I will then also make a diversion to Mr. Gene Bucks and see if I can get that book.

Yours,

Dear Ring:

Here is a copy of a letter I must answer. Shall I write to them that it is out of the question? I know you would not think of doing it, but I do not feel as if I ought t   'No" without authority.

I have been having a great time reading your s   icate articles;- have picked out quite a number on which I must get an estimate of the length, and shall go through again, to select more carefully. But there is certainly a great supply of most excellent material.

Have you ever read Voltaire's "Zadig and Other Romances"?

Yours,

The letter referred to is from Paul Elder and Company inquiring whether Lardner was available to speak in a series of celebrity lectures which was to include such names as Stephen Leacock and Lothrop Stoddard. Lardner always avoided such requests whenever possible.

From the magazine and newspaper articles Perkins was reading came *What of It?*, the volume of miscellany which Scribner's published in 1925. The book sold about 8,000 copies in the first year. Aside from *The Young Immigrunts* and *Symptoms of Being 35*, which were reprinted in the volume, it contains little worthy of critical study except the three remarkably contemporary "nonsense" plays—"Clemo Uti—'The Water Lilies,' " "I. Gaspiri," and "Taxidea Americana." These plays exhibit a kind of non-sequitor madness:

<blockquote>
Pat
I certainly feel sorry for people on the ocean tonight.
</blockquote>

Mike
What makes you
think so?
Pat
You can call me
whatever you like as long
as you don't call me down.

The characters in these plays talk, but
nobody listens to anyone else. It has
been suggested that such a mad world
reflects the deepening cynicism Lardner felt in his later years, and may
explain why Lardner felt unmotivated
to write the novel Perkins later continually urged him to do. Some lines in
these plays also have the definite bite
of the satirist; for instance, the following stage direction is obviously a criticism of stage "naturalism": "The curtain is lowered for seven days to de-
note the lapse of a week."

AUG. 29, 1924.

Dear Ring:

Did you ever discuss hay-fever in your syndicate?
Much could be said of it: I find I can still say much even
after the first two weeks. The wretched patient has publicly to
pretend he thinks it's funny too. If you consider the topic, I'll
submit myself, in the interests of science, to scrutiny.

Herein is a list of syndicate and other articles that seem
to me available for a book (title to be determined). I hope

you will recognize them from the list. I'll pick out others as the syndicate articles come in.

Scott said in a letter that came yesterday: "Seldes has been with me and he thinks, 'For the Grimalkins' is a wonderful title for Ring's book. Also, I've got great ideas about 'My Life and Loves' which I'll tell Ring when he comes over in September."

All right, but I'll go on along the present line, and if his plan is better, will change.

Yours,

P.S. I'm sending Voltaire's "Zadig". I read it in school; but I happened the other day to pick it up and *it* picked me up.

Gilbert Seldes was one of the prominent literary critics of the day, and one who evaluated Lardner's work with more perception than many. In addition to his post as literary critic for various New York newspapers, he served for a time in the 1920s as an associate editor of *Collier's* and then as managing editor of the *Dial.* He also wrote several books, the best known being *The Seven Lively Arts* (1924), a treatment of the popular arts. He edited both Lardner's posthumous *First and Last* for Scribner's in 1934 and *The Portable Ring Lardner* for the Viking Press in 1946.

Dear Ring:

There is, upon the whole, a very good review of "How to Write Short Stories" — it is rather an article about you than a review — in the September 3rd issue of the New Republic by Robert Littell. We just had this morning a very decent note from Bobbs Merrill which seems to open the door for a satisfactory outcome.

Yours,

In response to Perkins's request to purchase the rights to Lardner's earlier books, David L. Chambers of Bobbs-Merrill had in his reply reluctantly deferred to Perkins's request to sell the rights, plates, and stock on hand to Scribner's, so that Scribner's might publish Lardner's selected works as a set in 1925.

OCT. 2, 1924

Dear Ring:

This is to tell you that we have negotiated with Bobbs Merrill and with Doran and have acquired your books,- those of Bobbs Merrill for two thousand and that of Doran for five hundred dollars. In order to complete the transaction we must have a letter from you expressing your approval which we have told them we had, and I enclose a form which would be according to the usual practice, but can be varied of course, to suit your own taste. Now we will go over all the books and see what the best scheme would be. Apart from the set, of course we expect to carry them on our regular lists as trade books.

I enclose a new wrap on "How to Write Short Stories",- that is, new with respect to the back. I sent Scott a book which I hope you will see for I am sure you would like it, "Cowboys North and South" by Will James.

I hope Mrs. Lardner and you are having a splendid change and vacation. I found in the "Transatlantic Review" that extraordinary little play of yours[11] and I will hold that for the book.

Yours as ever,

Cowboys North and South was William Roderick James's first book, published by Scribner's in 1924. All of James's narratives of western life were tremendously popular. Among his other books were *The Drifting Cowboy* (1925), *Smoky* (1926), *Cow Country* (1927), *Sand* (1929), *Lone Cowboy: My Life Story* (1930), *Sun-Up* (1931), *Horses I've Known* (1940), and *The American Cowboy* (1942). James, who was a western rancher as well as writer, died in 1942.

11. "Taxidea Americana"

GREAT NECK, NEW YORK
NOVEMBER 11TH.

Dear Max:-

I enclose a letter to Bobbs Merrill as you requested.

I'm so desperately far behind in work that I don't believe I'll be able to get to town for a couple of weeks.

We had a pleasant session with the Fitzgeralds. Scott likes his new book, which he was revising when we left.

Sincerely,

Ring and Ellis Lardner vacationed in France in the fall of 1924. They left New York on 10 September, landed at Le Havre, and, after visits to Paris and Montpellier, visited Scott and Zelda Fitzgerald at St. Raphael. The group traveled by the Fitzgerald's auto to Monte Carlo where they won a moderate amount at the roulette wheel. The Lardners then returned to Paris, went on to London, and finally came home on the *Mauretania*. Lardner seems not to have been greatly impressed by Europe; his series for *Liberty* based on the trip is a burlesque of Twain's *The Innocents Abroad*, but it lacks the spontaneity of Twain's work. Even the visit with the Fitzgeralds may have been disappointing, since Lardner says little about it. Certainly it was during a trying period for the Fitzgeralds. Zelda's attraction at

St. Raphael to the French aviator
René Silvé had caused a crisis not fully
resolved by the time of the Lardners'
visit, and Scott in addition was busy
with revisions of *The Great Gatsby,*
which Scribner's published the following year.

Nov. 12, 1924

Dear Ring:

Thanks for your letter, and the one to Bobbs Merrill. I
know you must be in an awful jam,- even two weeks vacation for an office worker piles up the logs. But when you do
get clear, do let me know for we ought to get plans under
way. We are just printing a sixth 3000 of the book.

Yours,

Nov. 29, 1924

Dear Ring:

I'm delighted with Scott's book. It's got his old vitality,-
vitality enough to sweep away the faults you could, critically,
find with it;- which relate, in my view, chiefly to Gatsby
himself. Large parts of it are almost incredibly good and
there is in it a sort of strange mystical element which he has
not exhibited since "Paradise",- an element that comes
partly, perhaps, from once having been a Catholic. Well — I
am one of these 'jaded' readers, or ought to be and I read it

straight through and thought it much shorter than it was.

But what I meant to say in this letter was that we ought to get together, really, and I'll come to Great Neck if that would be easier. I hate to be a nuisance — I suppose you're harried to death — but we've started well and we ought to press the advantage.

If you haven't had time for "Three Flights Up"[12] do get Mrs. Lardner to read it. I *know* she will like it, especially the two stories in the middle.

Yours,

GREAT NECK, NEW YORK
DECEMBER SECOND.

Dear Max:-

I am tickled to death with your report on Scott's book. It's his pet and I believe he would take poison if it flopped.

Ellis and I have both read "Three Flights Up" and both liked the two middle stories best. My favorite is "Transatlantic." The last story is way over my head.

I think I am going to be able to sever connections with the daily cartoon early next month. This ought to leave me with plenty of time and it is my intention to write at least ten short stories a year. Whether I can do it or not, I don't know. I started one the other day and got through with about 700 words, which were so bad that I gave up. I seem to be out of the habit and it may take time to get back.

Don Stewart's "Mr. and Mrs. Haddock Abroad" was a blow to me. That is the kind of "novel" I had intended to write, but if I did it now, the boys would yell stop thief.

Five "articles" on the European trip are coming out in

12. By Sidney Coe Howard. Published by Scribner's in 1924.

Liberty, beginning in January.[13] I don't know whether or not they will be worth putting in a book.

I'm coming to town early next week to call on a dentist. As soon as I know when, I'll telephone you and try to make a date. Not that we don't want you in Great Neck, but I realize that it's no pleasure trip.

Sincerely,

Donald Ogden Stewart was an actor and writer of screenplays and humorous books, of which some of the latter became best sellers. He was also a friend of the Lardner family.

Dear Max:-

I enclose the pieces I think more worthy. I am sending the others in a separate envelope.

I have put new titles on the ones here enclosed, titles of which I am not proud, but which I believe are at least better than the Syndicate's. As soon as I think of a general title, I'll call you up.

It seems to me that the year and month when they were written ought to be put at the bottom or top of each piece.

Sincerely,

13. The five articles Lardner mentions appeared in the 14, 21, and 28 February, 7 and 14 March issues of LIBERTY—all under the title "The Other Side."

No record survives of Lardner's preferences, but presumably they were the pieces which later appeared in *What of It?*

Robert E. Sherwood, to whom Lardner refers below, was a New York playwright, a drama critic for *Vanity Fair* in 1919-20, and an editor of *Life* magazine from 1920 through 1928. Later, he was a speechwriter for Franklin D. Roosevelt, who appointed Sherwood special assistant to the Secretary of War. His three-act stage version of Lardner's "The Love Nest" achieved only indifferent results upon presentation in 1927.

DEC. 15, 1924

Dear Ring:

Bob Sherwood sent me the play from "Life" and "Liberty" has sent me proofs of the trip abroad articles, and I have got back from Hearst's those which they had run and I have had from you the *discarded* syndicate pieces. The others have not come and I hope the reason that you did not send them so soon is because you wanted to put titles on them. Otherwise we should have an awful time replacing them and ought to get at it as soon as possible.

Yours,

Dec. 17, 1924

Dear Ring:

I have just shaped up all the material to go in hand and I have arranged it in this way:-

1. "The Other Side" covered by a half title page with that phrase for a title.

2. The three plays (one still to come, but on the way) for which I haven't any half title, but should have one.

3. "Bedtime Stories" covered by a half title page under that phrase.

4. All the rest of the material beginning with "In Conference" covered by a half title page for which I have no half title, but which I have nicknamed "Obiter Dicta";- in fact, it did occur to us that if we called the whole book "Obiter Dicta" we would be making the same sort of title as that which we had on "How to Write Short Stories";- that is, we would be taking a shot at all these solemn literary collections of washed-out essays and comments and pedantic comments. Buy I gave that up because the words would mean almost nothing to so many people,- as a subtitle though it might do because those who saw the point would like it and those who did not, wouldn't bother about it one way or the other. This whole arrangement is subject to rearrangement, but it is good enough to start with.

Yours,

Dec. 19, 1924

Dear Ring:

Here is the memorandum of agreement for the new book. I simply designated it as "Bed Time Stories" because some phrase had to be used and that will serve the purpose of a contract. You will see we put the royalty at 15% from the start which is what it ought to be.

Yours,

Dear Ring:

I am sending you the wrap for the new book. A set of Scott's proof I have not yet been able to get because of the demand from the sales department, but I will send a set as soon as I can,- although I am almost tempted to wait until we get to the page proof stage, because Scott wrote yesterday in a letter that the number of corrections and changes and additions he was to make were such that I judge the whole book will have to be reset and will probably read quite differently even in detail. But if the corrected galleys do not come back soon, I will send you a set of the uncorrected.

I hope this design for a wrap will help you with the title.

This is a dismal black and white day here,- on account of a thin coating of snow, not whiskey. You're lucky to be where you are.

Yours,

The fact that Perkins would send Lardner a copy of Fitzgerald's proofs of *Gatsby* suggests both the closeness of Lardner's friendship with Fitzgerald and of Perkins's friendship with Lardner. Lardner proof-read the copy and suggested a few minor changes in descriptive details in the interest of more accurate representation of New York City. He explained his suggestions to Fitzgerald:

> I acted as volunteer proof reader and gave Max a brief list of what I thought were errata. On page 31 and 46 you spoke of the newsstand on the *lower level,* and the cold waiting room on the *lower level* of the Pennsylvania station. There ain't any lower level on that station and I suggested substitute terms for same. On page 82 you had the guy driving his car under the elevated at Astoria, which isn't Astoria, but Long Island City. On page 118 you had a tide in Lake Superior and on page 209 you had the Chicago, Milwaukee and St. Paul running out of the LaSalle Street Station. These things are trivial, but some of the critics pick on trivial errors for lack of anything else to pick on.

Dear Ring:

You may be troubled by the absence from the proofs of "Taxidea Americana". I hope you have not gone to the length of trying to get it yourself because I have got it now. It took a long time, but it is here and will be added in the proper place, that is, with the other plays. I wanted to scatter the plays more or less but I could not see how to do it and so in the end put them together. You must not hesitate to criticize anything with regard to the arrangement, etc., and in reading the proofs, do change those places which show that the material was first written for serialization,- not that we want to conceal this, but that we want the book to look up-to-date. I mean places where you speak of them as articles or refer to newspapers or magazines.

Sincerely yours,

Jan. 23, 1925

Dear Ring:

I know perfectly well that you have too much work to do already and my great desire is to do anything possible not to increase it needlessly in the hope of seeing you free to write stories,- or novels. Even now you are struggling to find a title — or have you found one? We have *got* to have it mighty soon. But couldn't you please write brief prefaces — a little over a page would do — on "Gullible's Travels," "You Know Me Al," and "The Big Town"? We are almost ready to issue them. I meant to ask outsiders to write introductions, but who could do it? There are only two or three people who could write good ones. I would not want to ask

Gilbert Seldes, for instance, because it would be absurd, nor Scott either, to tell the truth. The theory of an introduction is that the author needs somebody who is of higher standing than himself and you are not in a position where from this point of view anyone is available. Why should we ask Mencken to do it? It would be better to let them have their say when the books all come to them at once, and they can write something substantial. I wish you would do this.

I will send you Scott's proof as soon as I can get any of any sort, but if it is not until the page proof, you would be that much better off because Scott evidently plans practically to rewrite it.

Yours,

Perkins' frustration with Fitzgerald's continual revisions of *Gatsby* is evident here. Lardner later wrote to H. L. Mencken: "You have the right dope on the pains he took with Gatsby. He rewrote the whole book four or five times and had Scribner's crazy at the finish with revisions by cable."

THE NEW COLONIAL
NASSAU-BAHAMAS[14]
JANUARY 31, 1925.

Dear Max:-

How about WHAT OF IT? as a title. This is Grantland Rice's suggestion and it sounds pretty good to me.
I'll send you the prefaces in not too short a while.

14. The Lardners vacationed from January 13, 1925, through February in Miami and Nassau, in the company of the Grantland Rices.

Dear Ring:

"What of it?" is excellent, and already in process of stamping on cover and printing on wrap. Make any changes you want on page proofs, but quickly if you can manage.

Yours,

Dear Ring:

Herewith I am sending you the royalty reports on your book showing the sale since publication to February 1st. The first of these reports was due on November 10th, that is, six months after publication and should have been sent to you then; but I expected you here and asked that it be held, meaning to give it to you, and then failed to do so. But payment is now so nearly due on that first royalty report that we enclose our check for the amount called for. The payment on the other report as indicated at the foot of it, will not be due until the first of June, but if there should ever be any reason for your wanting it sooner we would be glad to pay it. The two reports together show a total sale to February first of 16325 copies;- but the sale seems to be continuing well and with the appearance of the new book and of the old books in a new way with your prefaces and all, it ought to continue to a much larger figure.

Now as to the set. According to our plan it is to consist of "You Know Me Al," "Gullible's Travels," "The Big Town," "How to Write Short Stories," and "What Of It". I tried hard to figure out another volume to be made up of such smaller material as "Symptoms of Being 35" and "The

Young Immigrunts" both of which seem to me admirable, and of "Say It with Oil" and the two war books. But the war books were very much objected to by the subscription department on the same old grounds that we are so tired of, and without the use of them it would be impossible to make up a book of the right size; moreover these sets ought not to run over five volumes and there was no disadvantage on the trade side in putting the new books in, and obviously a very considerable advantage. We therefore simply set aside these smaller writings in the hope that we shall be justified, as we very well may, in making up a volume of them later.

I do not know how familiar you are with the way these sets are sold. It is almost altogether by canvassers, though sometimes in part by mail order advertising and it is largely in combination with a subscription to the magazine. In view of the expense of collections and of the general machinery of selling, the margin of profit is a very low one, and therefore the terms given to authors are low, and may seem to you at first sight to be extremely so. We are ready to pay you the highest that we pay anyone, as we should do, which is a royalty of 20¢ per set; and this is to be paid according to the printing, and not according to the sale, and the first edition in this case would be 10,000 sets. The only special complication in the case is that we paid $2500 in taking over your books from the other publishers, $2000 to Bobbs Merill, and $500 to Doran. These were high prices in view of the fact that we virtually only purchased the rights in the plates, no stock to speak of that could be used. Do you think it would be fair, and we should not propose it unless we did, that half of this amount be set against your first royalties on this subscription edition? The other $1250 of course, to be borne altogether by us. We are, of course, issuing the three books also to the trade, and upon them we should pay the full 15% royalty, but how great their sale will be through the trade, in view of the appearance of the new books, is a good deal of a question, although it will certainly be much greater than it has been for some time while they were in the hands of the original publishers.

I have back some fifty galleys of Scott's book corrected, and not very largely changed so that it won't be long before we shall have a set of revised proof which I shall send you.

Yours,

Scribner's paid the George H. Doran Company $500 for the plates and rights of *You Know Me Al*, and $2000 to the Bobbs-Merrill Company for plates and rights of *Treat 'Em Rough, Own Your Own Home, The Young Immigrunts, Gullible's Travels, My Four Weeks in France, The Big Town, The Real Dope,* and *Symptoms of Being 35. You Know Me Al, Gullible's Travels,* and *The Big Town* were reissued under the Scribner's imprint in 1925, as part of a five-volume set, including *How To Write Short Stories* and *What of It?*

MARCH 11, 1925

Dear Ring:

"What Of It" is so much shorter than the other volumes which we plan to put into the set that we are adding to it "The Young Immigrunts" and "Symptoms of Being 35". I am delighted that the matter turned out this way because I thought those two were excellent and ought to be included, and yet I could see no way to manage it. I took it for granted that you would think well of this and that you would not need to read the proofs,- although you can if you wish, of course.

We are very anxious indeed to get the prefaces because we can publish with much greater effect if we can publish all the volumes in the trade at the same time. We can, for instance, get many window displays of great value.- But we cannot print the old books until we get the prefaces because the trade edition and the set edition will be printed together in every case excepting in that of "What Of It". So "anything you can do for us will be appreciated".

All of Scott's proof is now back and I shall soon be able to send you a final version partly in page proof, and partly in revised galley proof.

Yours,

Great Neck, New York
March 11, 1925.

Dear Max:-

The principal cause of delay has been lack of an idea. But I've also been fighting a cold; the kind that relieves you of all pep.

R.W.L.

Did you have the wrap changed on You Know Me Al?

Dear Ring:

I'm sorry for the cold. If you did these prefaces under that curse you performed a feat.

We have changed that wrap in respect to home plate with the help of Spaulding's latest guide and various authorities.

Yours,

Dear Ring:

I read "Hair Cut" on Friday and I can't shake it out of my mind;- in fact the impression it made has deepened with time. There's not a man alive who could have done better, that's certain.

Everyone will tell you this, or something like it I guess, so there's little use in my doing it.- But it is a most biting and revealing story and I'd like to say so.

Yours,

GREAT NECK, NEW YORK
MARCH SEVENTEENTH.

Dear Max:-

Thanks.

[57]

Perkins's judgment has been sustained. "Haircut" remains Lardner's most popular story today, and his most frequently anthologized piece. The story consists of the local barber's monologue about the town's practical joker, Jim Kendall, who emerges for us (but not for the unperceptive narrator) as a cruel and sadistic ne'er-do-well. The plot, which ends in the "accidental" shooting of Kendall by a mentally retarded boy whom Kendall has frequently ridiculed, is certainly melodramatic, but the essence of the story is in the technique of its telling, for the story is as much that of the barber as of Jim Kendall. The inadvertent revelation by the narrator of his own shallowness is an old device used extensively by Lardner as far back as *You Know Me Al,* but nowhere with more telling effect. The impact of "Haircut" depends on the reader's cognizance of the irony between the barber's insensitive interpretation and what actually happened. Curiously, Lardner had written no short stories between "The Golden Honeymoon" (1922) and "Haircut" (1925), an interval occupied by much talking about writing, people and events, by the writing of his Syndicate articles, by a good deal of drinking, and by much camaraderie with Fitzgerald and others. In 1925 and 1926, however, Lardner wrote twelve stories, nine of which were published in *The Love Nest and Other Stories* (1926), after having appeared individually in *Cosmopolitan* and *Liberty.* Perhaps the reason for Lardner's renewed vigor in 1925, in the writing of fiction, was that Ray Long, editor of *Cosmopolitan,* had in 1924 made him this offer: "For your next six short stories, $3000 each, or, for your next twelve short stories, to be delivered at intervals of not more than 45 days, $3500 each" (see Donald Elder, *Ring Lardner,* New York, 1956, p. 219).

Dear Ring:

I'm sending "The Great Gatsby". Will you some day return it? And, by the way: do you happen to have any snapshot of Scott or any picture of him you could lend, that has not been used? I suppose not, but thought possibly you might.

Yours,

GREAT NECK, NEW YORK
MARCH 19TH.

Dear Max:-

Thanks for the Gatsby proofs.

I'm sorry to say we haven't a picture of Scott; at least we can't find one. You might be able to get the one the Times ran a week ago last Sunday, or the one the Tribune had on a Sunday three or four weeks ago. These were taken in Rome and were in the rotogravure sections.

MARCH 19, 1925

Dear Ring:

Would you consent to coming here to sit for a few minutes for an artist if we could arrange for it very soon? We have a good one in mind and if we could get a drawing it would be much better than a photograph,- particularly as we have used the photographs we have a good deal.

Yours,

MARCH 20, 1925

Dear Ring:

Here are the prefaces. Will you hurry them back? And having added "The Young Immigrunts" and "Thirty-five" to "What Of It" we'd be infinitely obliged for any prefatory comments on that volume in the set.

Yours,

MARCH 26, 1925

Dear Ring:

"Time" will ask you to let them take a small movie of you, the pictures of which will be printed in strips in that magazine;- and they have asked us to back up the request which, as they are friends, and as we believe in the publicity, we hereby do.- But you know the desirability of it as well as anyone and will decide as you please when they ask you.

I just left Roy Durstine who had read "Hair Cut" and spoke of it in terms of utmost admiration.

Yours,

APRIL 1, 1925

Dear Ring:

I am sending you certain excerpts from that letter I wrote you about the set which in the form of a memorandum may serve as a sufficient contract if you will write on the bottom of it, "I agree to the terms as stated above" and simply sign it.

I could not overstate my hope that you will be able to do enough stories for a book this fall. I would come at exactly the right time and we should be in a position to feature it all through the season.

Yours,

MARCH 31, 1925

Memorandum of terms for the publication of
a subscription set.

As to the set: according to our plan it is to consist of "You Know Me Al," "Gullible's Travels," "The Big Town," "How to Write Short Stories," and "What of It" to which will be added "The Young Immigrunts" and "Symptoms of Being 35". We are ready to pay you the highest that we pay anyone, as we should do, which is a royalty of 20¢ per set; and this is to be paid according to the printing, and not according to the sale, and the first edition in this case would be 10,000 sets. The only special complication in the case is that we paid $2500 in taking over your books from the other publishers, $2000 to Bobbs Merrill, and $500 to Doran. These were high prices in view of the fact that we virtually only purchased the rights in the plates, no stock to speak of that could be used. Do you think it would be fair, and we should not propose it unless we did, that half of this amount be set against your first royalties on this subscription edition? The other $1250 of course, to be borne altogether by us. We are, of course, issuing the three books also to the trade, and upon them we should pay the full 15% royalty.

April 7, 1925

Dear Ring:

"What of it?" comes out on Friday. I'm sending you the usual six copies;- if you want more tell us so. And I'm sending two copies of each of the other books.

Yours,

GREAT NECK, NEW YORK
APRIL 18, 1925.

Dear Max:-

I want my brothers and sisters to have a full set of my books in the uniform edition. Will you please have Scribner's send a set to each of the following:

Miss Lena Lardner,
815 Bond Street,
Niles, Michigan.

Mrs. Richard G. Tobin,
815 Bond Street,
Niles, Michigan.

Mr. Henry Lardner,
898 South Third Street,
Niles, Michigan.

Mr. William P. Lardner,
9 Dodge Block,
Duluth, Minnesota.

Mr. Rex Lardner,
Great Neck, Long Island.

I'll be ever so much obliged to you. The bill may be sent to me or the amount charged to my royalty account.

The movie people were out this morning and I don't know who enjoyed it most, they or we.

APRIL 21, 1925

Dear Ring:

I'm sending the five books to each of those whose names you give in your letter. I haven't been notifying you of reviews for they must come your way — the leader for instance, in the New Republic Literary Supplement on spring books, by Bob Littell — but who would have thought Henry Stuart, an Englishman, newly arrived, would have done you so proud as that in the Times?

I've been telling movie people they ought to look into "The Big Town" myself.

What about that World review of "The Great Gatsby"?
Dismissed it with a paragraph! I understand the writer's
name is Saltpeter.[15]

Yours,

John N. Wheeler, of whom Perkins speaks below, was a former baseball reporter who had established the
Bell Syndicate, and who later became
editor of *Liberty.* He was a neighbor
and intimate friend of Lardner at East
Hampton. Lardner always had merely
a verbal contract with Wheeler to write
for the Bell Syndicate, and when
Wheeler and Lardner's brother Rex
were removed, late in 1925, as editors
of *Liberty,* Lardner took his stories to
Ray Long at *Cosmopolitan.* The three
stories of which Perkins had just heard
were probably "Mr. and Mrs. Fix-It,"
"Women," and "A Day with Conrad
Green," which were published in the 9
May, 20 June, and 3 October issues of
Liberty, respectively. All the other stories that later appeared in *The Love
Nest,* except "Reunion" which was
published in the 31 October *Liberty,*
were sold to *Cosmopolitan.*

15. Harry Saltpeter, a literary critic for various New York newspapers. His
article "The Boswell of New York" in the July 1930 BOOKMAN discusses his
interviews with many authors, including Lardner.

Dear Ring:

I just ran into John Wheeler at lunch and he told me of two stories written and one in early expectation. These with "Hair Cut" make four. In "How to Write Short Stories" we had ten, but we would not need quite that many for another book and what Wheeler said was encouraging. If we get out a book in the fall, we ought to put it in hand not later at the utmost than the first of August. Do you think that would be possible? If you do and if a title could be produced, I would start right away on a dummy, using the beginning of "Hair Cut" for the text of it. This fall would certainly be the right moment to put a new book of stories into the field.

Yours,

P.S. Very good reviews are coming out now about "The Great Gatsby" and better ones I think are to follow. We are beginning to receive reorders from Womrath in increasing numbers which is a good sign, of course.

Great Neck, New York
April 25th.

Dear Max:-

I do think there ought to be at least nine stories in a book and I am fairly well on the way to that number. Besides Haircut, Mr. and Mrs. Fix-it, and Women (a baseball story) for Liberty, Ray Long has two stories—Zone of Quiet (which, I think, will be in June Cosmopolitan) and The Love Nest (which I sent him this week). I intend to have one and possibly two more done for Liberty by the end of May. The quality of the five already written averages better than the stories in How To Write Short Stories and if we give 'em fair quantity too, they ought to be satisfied.

I'm glad to hear that Scott's book is going.

MAY 6, 1925

Dear Ring:

Did you ever write out a biographical sketch? We need one badly for our agents, etc. Anything you may have we could, I imagine, adjust, and if you have nothing couldn't you run something off?

Louise[16] told me she saw you and thought you looked well,- much better than a year ago.

Yours,

Lardner's health was failing as early as 1925, due in part, no doubt, to his drinking habits extending back to his early newspaper days. In 1926 his illness was diagnosed as tuberculosis, and although it was apparently arrested by a hospital stay in that year, Lardner suffered intermittently from the disease for the rest of his life. The winter "vacations" and extended rest periods in hospitals in later years were necessitated by Lardner's deteriorating physical condition, until his death on 25 September 1933.

16. Mrs. Perkins.

HOW TO WRITE SHORT STORIES

[WITH SAMPLES]

BY

RING W. LARDNER

NEW YORK

CHARLES SCRIBNER'S SONS

MCMXXV

Dear Ring:

I am sending you the check called for by the second royalty report on "How to Write Short Stories" which was sent you on February first. Everything goes well. Mencken had an excellent article in his syndicate. I saw Stuart who wrote in the Times, the other night, and he could have written another review quite as enthusiastic on an altogether new set of excellencies.- But he told me that the Times had received a number of indignant letters from old readers who said they could not understand such an article on a writer who did not even know *grammar.* I think they even went so far as to say you did not know how to spell. This is a grand world.

Scott has got magnificent reviews but his book is not selling properly. I really think his personal reputation has injured his books. That has given him an altogether frivolous look in the eyes of the trade and the public. They will not take him seriously and viewed as a jazz writer pure and simple, he seems an old story. But the book sells right along and may come out reasonably well. At all events it has certainly placed Scott higher than he was with the critical crowd, and the impression will gradually percolate through the public generally.

How are you coming on with the stories? Let me know some time. The sale of "What of It" to date is about six thousand.

Whether it is Mr. Coolidge's fault or not, the book business is suffering like all the others,- one of the flatest seasons in years.

Yours,

Lardner's skill as a recorder of the diction and the rhythms of the American language was far more precise than most people realize today, though in his own time even Carl Van Doren, who criticized Lardner's fictional characters for never "growing" or "becoming" (Van Doren failed to recognize that the static character is often an effective satiric device; e.g. Sinclair Lewis's George Babbitt), recognized his excellence as a "comic philologist." Lardner was often associated, especially by H. L. Mencken, with Mark Twain, since both men wrote the dialects of uneducated people. But Twain's Mississippi dialects of thirty years before were much different from the speech of Lardner's lower and middle class American "boobs" of the 1910s and 1920s. "I don't know his people," Lardner once said of Twain's fictional world. The precision of Lardner's scrutiny of the common American's careless speech is.clear in his 1921 review of J. V. A. Weaver's book, *In American,* a review so entertaining that I quote from it extensively:

> We can't hope to land the old K.O. on the writer's jaw, but we can fret him a little with a few pokes to the ear.
> For the most part this organ has served Mr. Weaver well. But I think that on occasion it consciously or unconsciously plays him false. It has told him, for example, that we

say *everythin'* and *anythin'*. We don't. We say *somethin'* and *nothin'*, but we say *anything* and *everything*. There appears to be somethin' about the *y* near the middle of both these words that impels us to acknowledge the *g* on the end of them. Mr. Weaver's ear has also give or gave (not gi'n) him a bum hunch on *thing* itself. It has told him to make it *thin'*. But it's a real effort to drop the *g* off this little word and, as a rule, our language is not looking for trouble. His ear has gone wrong on the American *fellow, kind of,* and *sort of.* Only on the stage or in "comic strips" do we use *feller, kinder,* and *sorter. Kinda* and *sorta* are what us common fellas say.

And how about the lines, "Now that I'm sure he never won't come back" and "You don't know how to dream and never won't?" *Never will* and *won't never* are American. *Never won't* ain't. Other lines I challenge are, "I crope up on him" and "You should of hearn the row there was." I don't say *crope* and *hearn* are impossible. I do say *crep'* and *heard* are a great deal more common.

The line, "Look what I done for you and him and me", is good American, but better American, I believe, would be, "Look what I done for him and you and I". This however brings up a subject to which one ought to be able to devote a whole volume, but one ain't goin' to. One is only goin' to state that mysterious rules govern the cases of personal pronouns in our language and one hasn't had time to solve the mysteries even since prohibition. We say, "He come up to me in the club", but we also say, "He come up to Charley and I in the club" or even "He come up to I and Charley in the club." Charley's presence in the club seems, for "some reason another", to alter my case. The other night I was reading a play script by one of this country's foremost dramatists; and recurring in it was the stage direction, "A look passes between he and So-and-So." But this playwright wouldn't think of saying or writing, "She passed he a look."

My theory on this particular point is that when the common American citizen, whom we will call Joe, was in his last year in school (the sixth grade), the teacher asked him how many boys there were in his family. He replied: "Just Frank and me." "Just Frank and I," corrected the teacher. And the correction got Joe all balled up.

The Great Gatsby, published 10
April 1925, generally received the best
critical reviews Fitzgerald ever got, but
the sales were disappointing by Fitzgerald's standards—just over 20,000
copies in the first year—perhaps, as
Perkins thought, because the public
reacted negatively to the brevity of the
book compared with the lengths of
Fitzgerald's previous volumes.

‣JUNE 19, 1925

Dear Ring:

I wish you would write me a letter, or better still, come
in and see me, or let me come and see you, to find out how
matters are progressing. The last thing I want to do is to give
you any sense of being pushed in the matter of the stories.
All I want is to find out how the chances are,- and if they are
not good we will simply wait until later.

I am sending you a set of the books in what is known as
"The Artcraft Edition" because of the binding. The binding
is called Artcraft leather which has at first a certain aroma;
but it gets over that after a little. The reason we have this
edition is because the binding has a very strong general
appeal apparently,- at least we have found it so with Train's
District Attorney set,[17] etc.

Gatsby has reached the point of 15,000 only. It sells
right along, but it evidently is not going to have a truly big
sale,- to that we shall have to make up our minds. I tell you
this in confidence, because it is not good for a book to have it
known that it is not selling as well as its predecessors.- But
Scott, I judge by his letters, is in good form, and much

---

17. Arthur Train, a lawyer himself, is best remembered for his Ephraim Tutt
stories about the achievements of a criminal defense lawyer.

pleased by the reviews, and by the appreciation of the Paris crowd, including one Hemingway whom he admires.

Yours,

P.S. We are publishing a book of his stories this fall,- "All the Sad Young Men".

In Paris Fitzgerald had become good friends with Hemingway by the summer of 1925. He had recommended Hemingway during the winter of 1924-1925 to a number of people, including Perkins, and he had persuaded Hemingway to offer *The Torrents of Spring* to Scribner's after Boni & Liveright had rejected it (the novel is a parody of the style of Sherwood Anderson, whom Boni & Liveright published). Fitzgerald's efforts on behalf of Hemingway were, as was the case with Lardner and others previously, simply the results of his sincere and unselfish enthusiasm about the quality of Hemingway's work. Fitzgerald never changed his mind about Hemingway the writer, though the two became less friendly later.

Dear Ring:

I'm always pressing writers, for copy, but somehow when I come to you I feel ashamed,- as if I were a dunn. But I'm asking at the moment for a very little thing,- a title. If you can produce that we can get up the inevitable dummn in time for the salesmen's principal fall trip. Have you thought of one?

Yours,

Dear Ring:

I have got together the stories you named except "A Day with Conrad Green" which Liberty will send me, and have made the following estimate upon them:

Mr. and Mrs. Fix-it,	4935 words
Women	5000 "
Haircut	5230 "
Zone of Quiet	5575 "
The Love Nest	5800 "
	26540 "

Allowing for 12,000 more words from "A Day with Conrad Green" and the seventh story, we should only have 38,540 words in all. The temptation is to get the book out on this basis and it is certainly very hard for me to resist it, because I think the stories almost incredibly good. "The Love Nest" is a marvel. But I do honestly think from a farsighted view, that we should act more wisely if we waited — and after all, it would mean only four months — until you had several more stories, so that the book would not look slim and perhaps padded, in half titles, etc. and a widely spaced page and all, along side of "How to Write Short Stories". It is bound to be compared with that and the fact that it was its equal in quality would not overcome the fact that it was not its equal in quantity,- at least it would not in the eyes of the trade:- they began by washing their hands of the whole matter when they saw how few pages there were in "The Great Gatsby" compared with his other books.

You suggested including "The Young Immigrunts" which in the specially bound set is included in the volume "What Of It?". But I do not think in this book, which is to be compared with "How to Write", there ought to be anything that is not a story, and certainly not anything that is not new, because it gives an impression that we try to hurry books into the market for the occasion.

We will do exactly what you say, but I ought to tell you exactly how it seems to me, and that is, that we should wait until February, when you would have enough more stories (wouldn't you?) to make a book of 60,000 words anyhow, which would be sufficient, and if those stories are as good as these, what a book it will be!

Yours,

Sept. 10, 1925

Dear Ring:

I am sending you herewith your royalty report. The payment is not due for four months and I suppose you will not object to our deferring it until then although if you should want the money for any reason, we would wish to send it. The sale of "How to Write Short Stories" must now total about 19,000 and it goes on steadily,- the fall orders have been good. The sale of "What Of It?" comes now to very little short of 7,000 copies, and the reorders for it too are good, although of course its sale as that of another sort of book must always fall behind the other.

The statements of sales on the old books are the individual sales, entirely apart from the subscription edition. I do not know just why "Gullible's Travels" should be in excess of "You Know Me Al" and "The Big Town", but so it is.

I am sending you a book that you may like called "Highland Annals".[18] In fact I know you will like it in some respects. I hope you are writing some stories. It would make things move when the next collection comes out.

Yours,

Dear Ring:

At last I think I shall be able to put before you a proposition for the publication of at least two of your books in England,- one, "How to Write Short Stories".

Hoping you have found time to write some more short stories, I am,

Yours,

P.S. Scott is getting on with a novel called "Our Type" but he has told me very little about it. "Gatsby" has sold about 20,000, but it still sells.

18. A collection of essays by Mrs. Olive Tilford Dargan. Published by Scribner's in 1925.

Dear Ring:

This is the proposition from Chatto & Windus, very good English publishers:-

They are prepared to purchase the rights of "How to Write Short Stories" and "Gullible's Travels" for the British Empire, except Canada, on the following terms: 10% on the first thousand copies, 12 1/2% on the next two thousand copies sold, and 15% thereafter; and they will pay on publication an advance upon the number of copies sold to the trade at that date; on cheap reprint editions which they issue they will pay 10%, and on cheap editions sold by them in the colonies, they will pay 5%.

This offer is dependent upon their having an option on "The Big Town," "What Of It," and "You Know Me Al," on the same terms; but this option must be exercised within twelve months after the publication of "How to Write Short Stories" which will be the first one to come out.

They also ask for an option on your next three books, but this is not important because the terms are not to be specified in advance, but are to be arranged in each instance. If you were dissatisfied with them by that time, you would rightly not come to terms with them.

Chatto & Windus are publishers of excellent standing. They are a fairly young house, and a lively one, and yet they are firmly established and so can give your books proper attention and representation.

All this we put before you for decision, but our opinion is favorable, and we can give it without any danger of partiality because we do not profit in any way by the transaction, except that any increase in your 'public' should have a favorable effect generally.

Let me hear from you soon about this, if you can.

Yours,

Oct. 12, 1925

Dear Ring:

I am letting Chatto & Windus think that we have every
expectation of your approving their offer, and I suppose they
will go ahead with their plans; but they won't go too far to
break off if you do not approve, so give me a final word when
you get through with the world series.

I am sending you herewith the royalty report on "What
Of It?"

Mrs. Lardner told me that she thought you had surely
enough stories ready for the book. I am delighted. Everything
is set for a real success for it. We should bring it out if
possible early in March, which would mean that we should
begin setting it up by the first of January.

Yours,

The World Series of 1925 was a
rather disastrous one for Lardner,
whose enthusiasm for this sports event
had been dulled by the sickening experience of the Black Sox scandal of
1919. The following paragraph from a
letter to Fitzgerald reveals why Lardner was tardy in communicating his
approval of Chatto & Windus to
Perkins:

I had forgotten what
terrible things world's series
were so I consented to
cover this year's. I got
drunk three days before it
started in the hope and be-
lief that I would be re-

morseful and sober by the
time I had to go to it. But
when I got to Pittsburgh it
seemed that I was the only
newspaper man in America
who had reserved a room;
all the others moved in with
me and there wasn't a
chance to eat, sleep, work,
or do anything but drink.
The result was two fairly
good stories and seven terrible ones out of a possible
nine, including rainy days.

Oct. 29, 1925

Dear Ring:

Consider whether we would not be doing a very good
thing by calling it "The Love Nest and Other Stories";- I say
"The Love Nest" because I think take it all round, it is about
the best one of the collection. The fact that a popular song
was so entitled might even be an advantage. But wouldn't
this type of title show up well in contrast with "How to Write
Short Stories", and would it not bring out in a most emphatic
way, the strongest point in favor of a book by you, that it is
made up of short stories? In this way too, we would avoid
any confusion with the other sort of collection represented by
"What Of It?". I am inclined to think that for once in the
history of publishing, this sort of title would be the best we
could get. How about it?

Yours,

Dear Max:-

I think your title is all right. It would be better, I
believe, to have a straight title like that instead of a trick title,
this time.

Have you Scott's up-to-date address? The last I have is
14 rue de Tilsitt, but he said something in his last letter about
moving. I hate to write a 1,500 -word news letter to him and
have it go astray.

Nov. 2, 1925

Dear Ring:

I think 14 rue de Tilsitt must be right for Scott, because
I got a letter from him just the day after we were talking, with
that address plainly written at the top.

We will now go ahead with the dummy and wrap, etc.,
on the basis of the title suggested.

Sincerely yours,

P.S. I hope your letter to Scott will cheer him up for he signs
his letter to me "somewhat mournfully". He is not in a very
good financial situation, I suppose, but otherwise he ought
not to be mournful. "The Great Gatsby" was a triumph and
greatly strengthened his position, and he has got some most
excellent stories in his next book, better than any he ever did.
He says he is getting on well with his new novel.

Following *The Great Gatsby,*
Fitzgerald's next volume was *All the
Sad Young Men,* published in 1926.
The volume contained "The Rich
Boy," "Winter Dreams," "The Baby
Party," "Absolution," "Rags Martin-
Jones and the Pr-nce of W-les," "The
Adjuster," "Hot and Cold Blood,"
" 'The Sensible Thing,' " and "Gret-
chen's Forty Winks." Perkins's praise
is deserved, for Fitzgerald had care-
fully selected the best nine of the
twenty-two short stories he had pub-
lished in magazines since his previous
collection, *Tales of the Jazz Age*
(1922).

However, Fitzgerald's communi-
cations to Perkins were misleading. In
the summer of 1925 Fitzgerald and
Zelda became enmeshed in a stream of
parties in Paris and London, and Fitzgerald actually wrote very little. The
projected novel to which Perkins refers
was "Our Type," a story of matricide
on which Fitzgerald worked intermittently for three years before he abandoned it in 1929.

DEC. 2, 1925

Dear Ring:

I am sending you herewith the check that is due according to your last royalty report,- $1608.68, and I am also
sending a proof of the wrap for the new book of stories.

There is a man in town I would greatly like to have you
meet,- Will James, who taught himself to draw and write,

and whose two books we have published. I am sending you the second. I think I did send you "Cowboys North and South". Your boys will like "The Drifting Cowboy" even if you do not get a chance to read it. But if you are to be around New York in the next several weeks, in a way which would make it possible, I wish you would let me know, because I could get James to lunch at any time you could come. He is a mighty intelligent fellow, and I believe you would like him.

As ever,

GREAT NECK, NEW YORK
DECEMBER 4, 1925.

Dear Max:-

Thanks for the check and the wrap, both of which looked good.

I'd like to meet Mr. James, but it will have to be a little later; I've promised to do a stunt for the Actors' Theater and have sworn an oath not to leave this house for immoral purposes till it is completed.

R.W.L.

Ray Long now has my last story—"Rhythm"—which will be in April Cosmopolitan, out March 10.

"Rhythm" is a biographically significant story, coming at this time,

THE LOVE NEST
AND OTHER STORIES

BY

RING W. LARDNER

WITH AN INTRODUCTION

BY

SARAH E. SPOOLDRIPPER

NEW YORK

CHARLES SCRIBNER'S SONS

MCMXXVI

when Lardner was deeply involved in the Broadway musical world. The protagonist, Harry Hart, is a song writer who is very nearly ruined when he is taken seriously by the critics. At first, Harry is a great popular success, plagiarizing operas and symphonies for his tunes. But when he is discovered by Spencer Deal, a serious critic, who proclaims Harry "the pioneer in a new American jazz," Harry begins to take himself seriously, with disastrous results. He drops his old friends, including his fiancée, and writes a moderately successful symphony (which nets him fifty-six dollars). After other "artistic" attempts, Harry, nearly broke, goes back to writing hit songs and effects a reunion with his girl.

The "stunt" to which Lardner refers earlier in the letter was Offenbach's "Orpheus in the Underworld," which Lardner was "Americanizing" for production by the Actors' Theater, with Otto Kahn's backing and Max Reinhardt directing. The modernization of Orpheus into a Tin Pan Alley song writer and Eurydice into a bored wife who wants out of the marriage did not work, however, though some of the lyrics are witty. The musical was not produced.

Dear Ring:

I am sending you the usual memorandum of agreement. I have read the last of the stories and I think it is a wonderful collection. Will you do the preface?— And the longer you make it, the better. Please do make it long if you can without forcing it. Say anything you want to. The stories add up to 46,200 words. I suppose the preface could easily make it 50,000, but even that is much shorter than the other book. It will do, however.- But if by some miracle you should have struck off another story in the interval between now and "Rhythm" the advantage would be great. There is the question too, of some possible notes and comments or little pieces you may have written — although I have not seen any — which could stand in italics on the back of half titles, and be inserted between stories. I suggest this simply in the idea that you may have something that would be just right for the purpose, or that you may think of something that would be just right. In any case it will be a most excellent book, but any additions to it would be so much the better.

Wishing you and Mrs. Lardner and all the boys [19] all the advantages of what are known as the holidays, and none of the disadvantages, I am,

Yours,

GREAT NECK, NEW YORK
DECEMBER 26, 1925.

Dear Max:-

I don't think there is a chance of my writing another

---

19. Ring and Ellis Lardner had four sons: John, born 4 May 1912; James, born 18 May 1914; Ring, Jr. (nicknamed Bill), born 19 August 1915; and David, born 11 March 1919. For an excellent commentary on the Lardner family, see Ring, Jr.'s "Ring Lardner and Sons," ESQUIRE, March 1972.

short story in time for publication before the book comes out. You see, I am now tied up pretty definitely with Cosmopolitan and it is already scheduling the July issue. I'll write as long a preface as I can. When do you have to have it? I can't think of any comments that would go between stories.

We had a merry, though dry, Christmas and hope you did, too (not necessarily dry).

Sincerely,

The preface to *The Love Nest* reflects a more definite cynicism and self-criticism than one finds in "Rhythm" or other earlier writings. Written by "Sarah Spooldripper" in the fashion of the introduction to *How To Write Short Stories*, it is simultaneously a parody on Mary Lawton's *A Lifetime with Mark Twain* (1925), a book narrating the experiences of Katy Leary as a servant in the Mark Twain household. More basically, it is a parody of all scholarly introductions. But when Lardner turns bitterly on himself, denying both his stature as a serious writer and his talent, the introduction becomes morbid rather than funny. "Sarah Spooldripper" writes as if Ring Lardner were already dead, and she closes her "eulogy" thus: "The Master is gone and the next question is who will succeed him? Perhaps some writer still unborn. Perhaps one who will never be born. That is what I hope."

Dec. 29, 1925

Dear Ring:

I did not suppose you could do another story. It was too much to ask. I think we will make out pretty well in quantity, and certainly we could not ask any more in quality. But I do hope the preface will be long, and that you will do it soon.

As ever,

P.S. Scott says the new novel proceeds slowly, but brilliantly.

GREAT NECK, NEW YORK
JANUARY 12,1926.

Dear Max:-

I am sorry to trouble you, but the Century Film Corporation which has bought the rights to my "busher" stories, says it is necessary, for the records at Washington, to have the enclosed assignment signed by Scribner's. Will you be good enough to have it signed and returned to Mr. Siegfried F. Hartman, 120 Broadway, New York?

Sincerely,

Dear Ring:

The first six galleys are on the way. If you have ideas on the order of stories, tell me. I've arranged them in a manner I thought appropriate, but without strong conviction. Now for the introduction!

As ever,

P.S. I suppose you'll see "Gatsby" on the 25th in Great Neck, and I'll run over to Stamford and see it on the 27th.

Owen Davis's dramatization of *The Great Gatsby* opened in New York on 2 February 1926 and ran successfully into the summer. Fitzgerald earned around $17,000 from his play rights, and at least another $15,000 when subsequently the movie rights were sold. James Rennie played Gatsby and Florence Eldridge, Daisy. The plot remained essentially faithful to that of the novel, though in the drama Wilson is cast as Tom Buchanan's chauffeur and, more significantly, Gatsby ultimately refuses Daisy as his mistress.

Jan. 20, 1926

Dear Ring:

I just called up, to find you were where you are. I hope you have had all the proof we have sent you, and will send it back soon with corrections, and that the introduction will be along.

Hoping that neither you nor Mrs. Lardner are in Florida for the sake of your health, but because you want to be there, I am,

Yours,

THE BELLEVIEW
BELLEAIR HEIGHTS, FLORIDA
JANUARY 25, 1926.

Dear Max:-

Several proofs have been forwarded to me down here. If it is all right with you, I will bring them, together with the preface, when I come up to New York, which will be about February 8. I'm going to be home two or three days and then set out again for New Orleans and California.

In the following letter the "assignments" Perkins mentions were contractual arrangements with the Century Film Corporation. Scribner's objected to the original contract assigning the motion picture rights to Lardner's Jack Keefe stories, on the grounds that the contract appeared to include even the rights of book publication. A substitute contract, drawn up by Scribner's counsel, was executed.

JAN. 28, 1926

Dear Ring:

If you bring all the proof of "The Love Nest and Other Stories" and the preface, on the 8th, all will be well. But for Heaven's sake make it not later than the 8th.

I had to get those assignments you sent me changed, before we could execute them, but this was done without any difficulty, and now the motion picture people have them. I do not see why they do not try "The Big Town".

I saw "The Great Gatsby" last night in Stamford and was really almost satisfied with it. The characters of Gatsby, Buchanan, and Tom are done as well as anybody could possibly hope they would be. The play is much more true to the book than I had any expectation of. As to whether it will succeed I haven't any idea, but nobody, including Scott, need feel ashamed of the play. That is certain. It makes an original and extremely effective presentation.

Yours,

Dear Ring:

I forget when you said you were going away, but I hope this check will reach you before you do. It is the royalty on "What Of It?" which we reported to you four months ago. I shall be sending you the royalty report on "How to Write Short Stories" in a day or so.

Yours,

March 2, 1926

Dear Ring:

I am sending you your royalty report. The payment will be due in June. I suppose you are perfectly willing to wait until then. I am enclosing herewith also, the spring list of Chatto & Windus. On page 11 thereof, you will find your name which will be followed by a general note and then by notes on the two books[20] they have taken. I thought this might interest you since these are your first English publications.

The play "Gatsby" is certainly making a success, and Scott must be now pretty nearly square with the world, financially.

Yours,

20. Gullible's Travels and How To Write Short Stories.

Dear Ring:

I do not know where you are, but I am sending half a dozen copies of "The Love Nest" to you at Great Neck and if you are not there I suppose they will wait for you. You noticed that Scott dedicated his "Sad Young Men" — which by the way, is getting excellent reviews and selling well — to Ring and Ellis Lardner.

I am sending along a very unusual book — "Fix Bayonets"[21] by Captain Thomason — which will certainly be appreciated by the four boys, anyhow.

Yours,

March 30, 1926

Dear Ring:

I called up your house to find that you were to be back on Sunday. We have an idea of making up a special little book to be given to the booksellers from your stories,- as what you might call a "souvenir" at the Booksellers' Convention in St. Louis. It would be strictly limited to a certain number of copies, and it should have a sort of introduction by you. You had such a bully introduction all ready for "How to Write Short Stories" that it occurred to me you might possibly have written something about books or something that would have some connection with booksellers in one of your syndicate articles. Anyhow I wish you could stop in here very soon for a few minutes, and let us tell you what the idea is.

I understand there is to be a very fine review of "The Love Nest" in the next week or so, in the Times.

Yours,

21. John W. Thomason, Jr.'s novel of the First World War was published by Scribner's early in 1926.

APRIL 10, 1926

Mr. Ring W. Lardner
Great Neck, Long Island, N.Y.

Find we need preface to souvenir book* for booksellers on Wednesday. Something about books booksellers writing or owning books. Will never forget your help if you can do this. Sorry to rush you.

Maxwell E. Perkins

APRIL 15, 1926

Dear Ring:

We want to use this in the book. Could you suggest a caption that Gene Buck would accept?

As ever,

JUNE 1, 1926

Dear Ring:

Here is the check that the last report called for. We'll do better for you next time.

Yours,

---

* CHARLES SCRIBNER'S SONS PRESENT RING W. LARDNER IN THE GOLDEN HONEYMOON AND HAIRCUT (St. Louis: American Booksellers Association; May 1926).

Dear Ring:

I am sending you one copy of the English edition of "Gullible's Travels" and one of the English edition of "How to Write Short Stories". I can send you half a dozen more of each if you want them. They have evidently just been published and I shall keep an eye open for English reviews and send you any of note.

It would be a great thing if you would write another long story like "Gullible's Travels" or even better, as long as "The Big Town", which could be published by itself. I suppose from a magazine standpoint it might not be profitable, but it would give a great chance to the book publisher.

Yours,

The "variety of documents" Perkins introduces in the letter below include a letter from Curtis Brown Ltd. to Scribner's, explaining that Curtis Brown had received a request by Dr. Arthur Rundt for permission to attempt to place the German serial rights to works by Ring Lardner, which the American Book Department had recently placed for Scribner's in London. Curtis Brown offers in the letter to negotiate the foreign rights for Lardner's work on the following terms: "10% on the price secured paid to our representative abroad, and our own commission of 10% . . . taken on the

amount received from him, making a
total of 19%." Eventually Dr. Rundt
did sell "Champion," in translation, to
three papers: *Prager Tagblatt, Tag* of
Vienna, and *Lokalanzeitung* of Dussel-
dorf, for a total of 180 marks, 90 of
which was paid to Lardner. Though
Rundt found it difficult to place Lardner's stories in Germany, "on account
of their extremely American atmo-
sphere," he requested and got from
Scribner's a promise that Scribner's
would not dispose of the German
rights of any of Lardner's work without informing him.

Dear Ring:

 I enclose for you a variety of documents. As for the
German arrangement, I think you had better let us tell Curtis
Brown to deal with the matter. You can hardly attend to it,
and we have not the connections that this agency has because the Continental market is outside of our rights. You
would probably make very little money out of the deal, but
so far as any results should come they would be advanta-
gèous. If this is your opinion send the two letters back and I
shall tell Curtis Brown to go ahead and shall send them Dr.
Rundt's letter.

 I was delighted this morning to find   fore me the first
chapter of your autobiography.- And this just when I had
begun to think that you ought to write something long

enough for publication as a unit, in one volume. For Heaven's sake keep it up to the length of twenty-five thousand words at least,- and the more beyond that, the better.

Yours,

The Story of a Wonder Man (1927), to which Perkins here alludes, is a parody of autobiographies in general and Lardner's in particular. Unfortunately, the published book, a collection of newspaper columns that appeared between July 1926 and January 1927, is a rather tedious one, made up of many bad puns and intentional irrelevancies in an effort, apparently, not only to bring the book up to the length Perkins desired but also perhaps to burlesque his own ability to communicate. This darkening cynical strain in Lardner's work is intensified by another of the "Sarah Spooldripper" introductions, which explains that the book "was written a chapter at a time and should be perused the same way with, say, a rest of from seven weeks to two months between chapters. It might even be advisable to read one chapter and then take the book back to the exchange desk, saying you had made a mistake."

Dear Max:-

Whatever arrangements are made with the German guy are all right with me, provided somebody tells him how to spell my name.

I'm afraid there isn't a chance of running the "autobiography" into anything like 25,000 words. The papers can use about eleven hundred words of it a week and if I extended it over ten or twelve weeks, it would get to be a terrible strain on both readers and writer. Couldn't it be used in a book along with the five or six short stories that will have been published by next winter?

Excuse the new ribbon.

JUNE 14, 1926

Dear Ring:

We'll see how the autobiography comes out, and I would be the last one to urge you to force it to an unnatural length, against your inclination. But if it should come to between twenty and twenty-five thousand, it could be published alone as a book and a continuous book always has an advantage. If it does not, it will do admirably if published in the lead of six or seven short stories.

Won't you please come in some day soon, when you are already in town? Mr. Bridges,[22] editor of Scribner's, is very anxious to see you.

Yours,

22. Robert Bridges, the poet and critic, was at this time editor of SCRIBNER'S MAGAZINE.

Nov. 18, 1926

Dear Ring:

I have been reading the Autobiography. Large parts of it are amazingly good. It does present the problem of continuous reading, but it seems to me a problem we will have to solve because it certainly ought to be published in book form somehow, either alone or with stories.

I have also read the three Cosmopolitan stories and I am going to get the fourth from Frazier Hunt. There are several points we ought to talk over. Couldn't we do it some day when you are in town? I would fit myself to any place or time you named, but I wish you would come and have lunch.

Yours,

The three stories to which Perkins alludes were "Rhythm," "Travelogue," and "I Can't Breathe," which appeared in the March, May, and September issues, respectively, of *Cosmopolitan.* The fourth story was "The Jade Necklace," which was published in the November *Cosmopolitan.* Frazier Hunt was an editor of that magazine.

Dear Ring:

I am pretty clear in my mind now that the autobiography ought to be published by itself, and with some sort of illustration. It ought to be published quickly too, for ever so many of its hits are of the moment.- So I wish we could talk it over soon.

Seldes called up and told me that Scott is really coming home in early December.

Yours,

The Fitzgeralds actually sailed for America from Genoa on 10 December, after two and a half years of many parties and much high living. Though Fitzgerald had continually assured Perkins that his new novel was coming along well, he had actually written very little, and they had saved no money, so he arrived back in America in a depressed state of mind. In December, when Perkins pressed him about the state of his work, Fitzgerald admitted that the novel was nowhere near completion.

DEC. 2, 1926

Dear Ring:

I enclose a check in payment of royalties now due on the sales of books up to August 2nd,- that is, four months ago. I have held this for a day or two, thinking that you would probably come in. If it would be easier for you, I could come down to Great Neck, but I could show you how we would illustrate the book, and that sort of thing, more satisfactorily in the office. We are all ready to go ahead and prepare the dummy as soon as we find that everything is right with you.

I got a letter from Scott several days ago, asking me to lunch with him in New York on December 20th. He has evidently engaged his passage and is sure to come. He says his book is not nearly ready.

I am sending a book called "Smoky"[23] to the youngest member of your family, although I believe it would be liked as much by the oldest.

Yours,

DEC. 8, 1926

Dear Ring:

I'll tell you what I have done. We are preparing a dummy on the Autobiography — and by the way, tell me the exact title — with an illustrated wrap, and with some illustrations, and they are using a part of the text. I felt we could not postpone this because dummies do make a great difference in presenting the book to the trade. As to the actual text, there are certain chapters which I thought we might omit, partly because they were more or less similar to others in effect, and partly because once or twice, I did not think they were as good as others. You are by far the best judge of what should go in and what should go out, of course, and are the sole authority on the question. If you think I am wrong, you

23. By Will James.

naturally will tell me, and we will put back those articles after we read the proof. Then, I think if you will feel as free as possible to edit the proof, and will do it with reference to time, because that makes a difference in a good many of the points, we shall perhaps do just as well as we might have done by discussing the manuscript in advance. We shall give the printer extra work, but we shall have to face that, and we are quite ready to do it.

I should like to show you the wrap material and the pictures some time, but it is not so important if you have enough confidence in us to do well in these respects. The only thing is that you could give great assistance to us.

I just read with great delight, in the Cosmo, the story "Sun Cure". But I think the best of the four is "The Jade Necklace" which is perfect. I wish though, that for the next book of stories, we could have one long one, and the longer the better. I know that while you are writing for the Cosmopolitan, this is impossible for periodical use but couldn't you do one long one just for a book? If it were twenty or twenty-five thousand words, we would have something entirely new, and we could make ever so much of it, and we might be able to even get a financial return that would warrant the sacrifice of magazine publication. I do not mean, of course, that you should deliberately think up a story for this purpose, but you may well have one that you want to write, and could write best at that length. We could strike a new note for you then. It might be in the vein of "Champion", a sort of biography of a type of character. If you had an impulse to write a long story of this sort, I truly believe it would be a good thing to do, even if your agreement with the Cosmopolitan prevents its serial publication.

Yours,

This is one of several letters in which Perkins urges Lardner to write a long fictional work. Perkins hoped that Lardner was capable of producing a humorous novel, in the Twain tradition, of baseball life or the broader panorama of lower middle class America. What is most curious about such comments (which were made fairly frequently, and not just by Perkins) is the non-recognition of *You Know Me Al,* which though a great popular success never drew much attention from literary critics, who were as little ready to accept baseball as a proper subject for literature as they had been earlier to regard seriously Mark Twain's narratives of life along the Mississippi River. This is not to say that *You Know Me Al* approximates a *Huckleberry Finn* or that Perkins himself did not appreciate fully Lardner's earlier work, but simply to point out that the epistolary bumblings of Jack Keefe deserved more critical attention than the book received in the 1920s, even after Scribner's reissued it in 1925. One exception, however, among the critics was Virginia Woolf, who discovered that in the book "the figure of the foolish, boastful, innocent athlete lives before us. As he babbles out his mind on paper there rise up friends, sweethearts, the scenery, town, and country—all surround him and make him up in his completeness. . . . Mr. Lardner at any rate provides something unique in its kind, something indigenous to the soil, which the traveller may carry off as a trophy to prove to

the incredulous that he has actually
been to America and found it a foreign
land."

Jan. 3, 1927

Dear Ring:

Please return the manuscript for "The Story of the
Wonder Man". I hate to be such a nuisance, but it is important.

As ever yours,

Great Neck, New York
Sunday.

Dear Max:-

Here is the introduction; also the manuscript, which I
have trimmed a little. And a copy of the contract. I'm sorry I
have kept you waiting, but I am helpless when my right arm
isn't working, as I simply cannot dictate.

As I told you, Chapters 1, 2, 3, 6, 22, 23, 26 and 27 are
missing from the manuscript. I think most of them can be
used with little alteration.

Jan. 10, 1927

Dear Ring:

I am sorry you had more trouble with your shoulder. I hope they have got it right now.

The manuscript came back O.K. and I found that in the end, after looking over what was already here, we only lacked chapters 3, 6, 22 and 23;- these the syndicate is sending me, and you can do anything you think right, in the proof. I cut out all the cross heads. I do not think they add much. I gave every chapter a title, but did it hastily and in the idea that you would probably give many chapters better titles. I am not under any illusions about myself as a humorist, at least. I believe we are going to have a splendid book.

Yours,

Perhaps Lardner's failure to do much in the way of revision of *The Story of a Wonder Man* stemmed from a realization that the manuscript was uneven, boring at times, and generally only a potboiler, in spite of Perkins's enthusiasm.

Jan. 18, 1927

Dear Ring:

Why don't you write about the boy who believed the 'ads'; read up on all the highbrow stuff and tried it on the gals!!- And the boy who didn't.

Yours,

Dear Max:-

That sounds like a good idea and I'll see some time what I can do with it. Thanks.

Sincerely,

There is no evidence to indicate that Lardner ever attempted to develop Perkins's plot suggestion; in any case it never resulted in a published story.

MARCH 3, 1927

Dear Ring:

I am sending herewith the royalty report on the sales within the last six months. I would like to have a long talk with you when you get back, about the possibility of a new book of stories which will contain several of a sort of biographical kind, and long ones. I believe we could do much better than we ever have done, with such a book.

"The Wonder Man" is on press, and will soon be on the bookstands. I hope all goes well with you all.

As ever,

Dear Ring:

When I sent you copies of "The Wonder Man" I thought you were still away, and so I did not write. I saw you at the Dutch Treat dinner. I had gone up to your box but there were a number of people there I didn't know, and I lost my nerve.

You always do everything your own way so perhaps you would rather not, but I wish I could sometime have a talk with you in the idea that you are now so much freer, that you might be willing to think of a book on a larger scale than you have done. The last thing I want to be is a nuisance, so if you would rather not, all right.

Jim Tully was just in here. He is anxious to see you, partly with a view to an interview, but partly because he always has wanted to. I told him I would ask you if you could manage it within the next several days. He said on Sunday afternoon he could go down to Great Neck, if it would suit you. He wants to do an interview for College Humor.

Yours,

Dear Ring:

Some day you ought to take a shot at the "Clean Desk" executive. The doctrine that the desk of the great executive is always *clean* has obsessed some of these gents to a point at which they simply sit behind a clean desk as if for a camera and admire the vacant landscape. I know one. He is always there behind this shining surface and he really can't do any work because he can't put anything on it,- except a telephone. He can only use it to pound when bullying his "producers".

The sale to date on "The Wonder Man" is 5290. It goes on quite well,- has been out six weeks. The reviewers didn't do very well by it in one sense.- They praised it highly, but they didn't handle it well, I thought.

I was thinking hazily of a book of biographical stories on the order of "Champion", perhaps; quite long — Lives of Great Men. Anyhow, if you ever feel like talking over a plan, give the signal, for I'm ready and anxious.

Yours,

Perkins's assessment of the reviewers is accurate. The reviews tended to be more favorable than the book deserved, and they tended also to talk more about Lardner in general as a humorist than about the book as parody, as self-parody, or as literature at all. The New York *Times Book Review,* for instance, praised Lardner's "knack of oblique humor": "Its freshness has not suffered through weekly exposure in a Sunday supplement and if there be criticism to make it is of a certain laziness and repetitiousness on the part of this talented humorist. For Mr. Lardner is a humorist, not a satirist, nor even an ironist: his humor is harsh, wry and at times savage, but it is diffuse. It lacks the sense of morality which animates satire. . . ."

Dear Ring:

Here is the check that is called for by the royalty report sent you four months ago.

Yours ever,

JULY 26, 1927

Dear Ring:

I have just recently got back from London. The sun never shone on the British possessions while I was there either. I saw Barrie, and he spoke with the greatest enthusiasm of you. He says he reads everything of yours he sees.

I do not want to bother you if you are writing a play, but I thought possibly you might be getting toward the end of that, and might be willing to think about a book. So if you are, tell me, but otherwise do not let this letter interrupt you.

I went over on the boat with Jack Wheeler and had a few talks with him, but he was all for health and exercise, and I was too sleepy to show much activity outside the smoking room.- So we saw not much of each other.

Yours,

Lardner was at this time collaborating with George M. Cohan on *Elmer the Great,* a three-act play based on Lardner's story, "Hurry Kane," about a baseball pitcher who, under the influence of a chorus girl, momentarily agrees to throw a Series for money. After openings earlier in the year in Boston and Chicago, it ran for a mere forty performances at the Lyceum Theater in the fall of 1928. Although Cohan and Lardner were good friends, Cohan did not understand Lardner's humor, and he chose to delete most of the subtleties in characterization (Elmer emerges in the play as the savior of the game) in order to develop a melodramatic role in which Walter Huston, who played Elmer, could display his acting abilities.

SEPT. 7, 1927

Dear Ring:

I am sending you the royalty report on sales to August first. Is there any chance of your doing some more long short stories now?

I hear Bob Sherwood has made a play of "The Love Nest" which I should think might make an excellent play.

Yours,

The plot of Sherwood's play remained essentially that of Lardner's story, except for the resolution where

the dipsomaniac Mrs. Gregg leaves her
overly possessive husband by eloping
with the butler. The play was not a
success; it ran only three weeks. Lardner foresaw the failure; he wrote to
Fitzgerald: "This ain't my play,
though of course I will share in the
receipts. (There won't be many.) I saw
a dress rehearsal last night. Bob has
done some very clever writing and the
second act is quite strong with June
Walker great as a drunk. But I'm
afraid most of it will be over people's
heads."

OCT. 11, 1927

Dear Ring:

I went down to Ellerslie Mansion week before last. I
think it is one of the most attractive houses I ever was in,
with the River at its back. I though Zelda was coming on in
great style, and she seemed very well too,- but Scott did not
seem at all well, and I have had him on my mind ever since. I
wish he would go to Muldoon or some such place for a
month to straighten out his nerves.

He read me from a letter of yours in which you said
your play was coming on. May it be a magnificant success!
But since it is written, and all the work done on it, I hoped
you might begin to think of a book. I have just bought a
number of the Cosmopolitan which has a story of yours in
it,[24] and I know there are others, and perhaps there are not
far from enough to make up another book of stories. The
only thing is that I had hoped we might work up a scheme
which would make a rather different book from "The Love

24. "The Venomous Viper of the Volga," in the September COSMOPOLITAN.

Nest". But it all depends upon what you feel disposed to do. I hope you can tell me.

I am sending you Hemingway's book[25] which comes out on Friday.

Ever yours,

Ellerslie was an old Greek-styled mansion outside Wilmington, Delaware, which the Fitzgeralds had leased in April 1927, after their return from Hollywood. United Artists had hired Fitzgerald to write the script for a comedy to star Constance Talmadge but the result, "Lipstick," was rejected. The Fitzgeralds then returned East, reportedly leaving a number of unpaid bills in California. Their private lives were turbulent at this time. Zelda had begun to exhibit traces of her later mental illness: at times, according to Fitzgerald, she spoke little, and at Ellerslie she developed an obsession with ballet dancing which lasted until her first mental breakdown in the spring of 1930. And Scott had become so involved, as usual, in the local social life that his resulting obligations rendered him unable to work on his novel as he wished.

25. Men Without Women

Dear Max:-

I am sorry to hear that Scott isn't well. I wouldn't recommend Muldoon's as a cure for nerves, especially Scott's kind of nerves. From what I have always heard, it is so strenuous that when a person is released, he is inclined to go on a bat to make up for it. I don't believe I have any influence over Scott, but I'll try to see him some time soon, either down there or here.

The play isn't finished. I have done it through the first time, but it is still to be torn to shreds by Cohan and done over again by him and me.

Cosmopolitan has enough stories, already printed or to be printed, to fill a book, but only about two of them are worth putting in a book. I'd rather wait until there are enough decent ones or until I've done something "different." If ever.

OCT. 20, 1927

Dear Ring:

Anyhow I am going to get together your stories from the Cosmopolitan and read them all, and be in a position to act however you may think right.

I can see that you will have to give lots more time to the play. I had an idea it was to be produced very soon, and I suppose it will be produced this fall.

Scott turned up here yesterday. His nerves are still in mighty bad shape (but don't say anything about it, perhaps especially to him, at least unless you do it verbally). The doctors tell him he must take exercise and must not drink, but that he is really O.K. in every important way. He worked here for an hour and then got one of his nervous fits, and could not work any more and wanted to go out and have a drink.– So we did it on condition that it would be one drink only, and that is all we had. I am sure anyhow, that if he will finish up his novel, which is about five thousand words from completion, and will then take a real rest and regular exercise, he will be in good shape again. We had a great talk over the drink. He is as good as ever except when he has a nervous fit.

Yours,

Lardner's stories appearing in *Cosmopolitan* since the publication of *The Love Nest* were "Travelogue" (May 1926), "I Can't Breathe" (September), "The Jade Necklace" (November), "Sun Cured" (January 1927), "Hurry Kane" (May), "Then and Now" (June), "The Spinning Wheel" (July), and "The Venomous Viper of the Volga" (September).

Dec. 16, 1927

Dear Ring:

I want to ask you in complete confidence both as to what I say, and as to what you say, about one matter. We publish for Bob Sherwood who made a play of your "Love Nest". Bob is sending it in with another play of his. He wants to publish the two in one volume this spring, and we would naturally want to do what he wants, assuming the plays are up to a certain level of quality, etc., of course. But before even reading the play I want to ask you how you feel in the matter. Bob said he was going to ask you, but I thought perhaps there might be something you could say to me more easily than to him.

As to your stories, I have read all of them, and taken a list of them and the dates of the numbers they appear in. Perhaps none of them equals "Some Like Them Cold," "The Love Nest," "The Golden Honeymoon," "Champion," or "Hair Cut". Nevertheless, they are (I think), in spite of what you said, very unusual stories, and they should certainly be published in a book,- and by next August you may have written one or two that do equal those I named, which seem to me your very highest points. Don't you think we could be thinking of a new collection for the fall? Among the new ones the story I liked least is "Man Not Overboard" and yet I know several people who think that wonderful.

I hope you are all keeping well in this rotten weather.

Ever yours,

These new stories to which Perkins alludes are effective but generally inferior to those printed in *How To Write Short Stories* and *The Love Nest.* There is little novelty; most are variations of earlier stories and themes. Lardner's favorite devices are repeated—the exchange of letters, the monologue, the diary, and the heavy emphasis on the dialogue of the common man. The settings are the baseball diamond, the card table, the golf course, the small town, the middle class home, the resort, and the Broadway producer's office. There is one shift in technique: ten of the sixteen new stories which appeared subsequently in *Round Up* are told in third person. A collective shift in tone is also noticeable. Bitterness and satire seem more heavily present because many characters are so disgusting as to totally lack human sympathy, while other characters are more pathetic than those of earlier stories. In "Contract," for instance, Mr. Shelton condemns the "educational complex" of bridge players: "It's a conviction of most bridge players, and some golf players, that God sent them into the world to teach." In "Nora," Mr. Hazlett, a musical comedy writer, endures the complete destruction of his play by a philistinic Broadway producer and his cohorts. The sentimental strain is evident particularly in two stories: "There Are Smiles" and "The Maysville Minstrel." In the former, Ben Collins, a semi-literate, good-natured traffic cop becomes infatuated with a pretty feminine speeder, Edith Dole, who represents an escape from a life and a marriage which Ben vaguely senses to be without purpose. When Edith dies in a traffic accident, Ben laments: "I can't feel as bad as I think I do. I only seen her four or five times. I can't really feel this bad." In "The Maysville Minstrel," the best of the new stories in *Round Up,* Stephen

Gale, a small-town bookkeeper for the gas company, is duped by a water heater salesman into believing that he can sell his homespun poems for a dollar a line. His realization that he has been tricked draws our sympathy because he has been led to believe for a time that he can escape the debt-ridden existence to which he is condemned. The story ends with Stephen's full realization that "there was nothing he could do about it."

GREAT NECK, NEW YORK
DECEMBER 17,1927.

Dear Max:-

I honestly haven't the slightest objection to your publishing "The Love Nest".

Some time this winter I may write one decent short story and if I do, we can talk about a book for next fall.

I thought Hemingway's book was great and am glad it went, and is going, well. Also that Scott is in better shape.

DEC. 20, 1927

Dear Ring:

Thanks for your letter. I hoped you would tell me whether you thought "The Love Nest" was a good play, and likely to be successful.- But these are questions which nobody perhaps can answer in advance of production.

I do wish you would write one long short story to head a book. I suppose this is hardly compatible with what you are now doing, (with the needs or whatever they are, of the Cosmopolitan). I am sure that these stories you have done will make an excellent collection, and all we need is one at your highest point to lead off.

The January Scribner's[26] comes out with a new cover and a new page, and I believe that the quality of its material will be better too. I hope you will look at it. I wish to thunder we could have a story by you, but we cannot touch your prices at present. If ever you write anything that does not somehow fit the Cosmo and such magazines, I hope you will remember us.

Yours,

MARCH 1, 1928

Dear Ring:

I have just read your story, "Liberty Hall" with a great deal of pleasure. I do truly think that these new short stories ought to be published in a book. There are now eleven of them that I have on my list and I think there are several that I have not got. You have probably written others too that have not yet appeared. If we could get out a volume of about fifteen of these short stories, it would be a very fine book I believe, and it would have a certain unity too, in tone and quality. It is now two years since you have published a book of short stories and it will be more than that by fall, which is the earliest that this one could come out.

I am enclosing herewith royalty report for sales in the last six months.[27] I have an idea that after a certain time we

26. SCRIBNER'S MAGAZINE.

27. The royalty report to which Perkins refers does not survive; however, Lardner's royalty check for 1 August 1927 was $1815.77.

might make up a selected volume from all these stories,- or else we might make a large collection containing all of them in one volume.- But for the present, it does seem to me that those you have now written would be an excellent collection, and that they ought to be brought out.

Yours as ever,

"Liberty Hall," published in the March 1928 *Cosmopolitan,* is another story about a writer of musicals, but here the objects of ridicule are the over-solicitious host and hostess, and Ben Drake, the writer, is a sympathetic character, attempting to hide from the demands of producers after a success-ful musical. Mrs. Drake, the narrator, is also a pleasant if slightly snobbish character; their happy marriage is one of the few in Lardner's fictional world. Lardner himself identified, one sus-pects, to a considerable degree with Ben Drake.

MARCH 21, 1928

Dear Ring:

I dare say you think I am worse than a man with a bill, but we are getting so near to the time when we must know our most conspicuous items for fall publication that I wish you would tell me if you do not think it wise to bring out a volume of stories. It would be a fine full volume of a very high order.

Yours ever,

Dear Ring:

We are again confronted by the inevitable dummy, and that means that we require a title. I thought we should make the jacket entirely different from the usual burlesque. What I should like to do would be to get some good phrase for a title that covered all the stories, and then to put a fine portrait of you right on the jacket, quite large. We have a good photograph, and could make such a picture from it, but it might be that somebody has made a very good drawing,- although I never saw one. Have you one?

Yours ever,

APRIL 18, 1928

Dear Ring:

Chatto & Windus were never able to educate the English public sufficiently in the American language to make your books successful. Now a young and new publisher, and well thought of, Philip Allan, wants to make a fresh attempt by combining "The Love Nest" and the sketches of "What Of It". He thinks this will give the book more volume and variety and he offers an accrued advance on account of 10% royalty to 2,500 copies sold, 15% to 10,000 and 20% thereafter for the British Empire except Canada volume rights. Of course this is not very attractive from a financial standpoint, but I would rather think the experiment worthwhile. Your books are so peculiarly American and about Americans that it would not be strange if they were not easily understood in England by the run of people. But if they are well published there, you may gain a public that will grow. Anyhow, let us know what you think so that we can answer the proposal.

I suppose you know Scott is going abroad on April 21st with Zelda, but only until about the middle of July. He certainly needs to make some kind of a change. He has been terribly depressed, and does not look at all well.

Send us a title soon.

Yours,

Fitzgerald had found it impossible to work consistently at Ellerslie on his novel; thus he and Zelda left again to spend the summer in Paris. This plan turned out disastrously, for Zelda's concentration on her dancing, now under the tutelage of Egarova, became a fixation, and Fitzgerald, sensing the widening gulf between them, drank a great deal, became noticeably more quarrelsome in public (twice landing in jail as a result), and accomplished little writing. They returned home to Ellerslie late in September.

Dear Max:

I am perfectly willing for you to try out Mr. Allan on the terms he offers. I saw Scott and Zelda about a week before they sailed. I will send you a title, as soon as I can think of one.

Sincerely,

MAY 25, 1928

Dear Ring:

I am sending you contracts for the stories. I have now all that have been published, including that one which appeared in the last Cosmopolitan.[28] There will be two more, will there not? I am ashamed to ask you for a title. I feel as if I ought to be able to suggest something myself. There are some mighty good individual titles on the stories, but it would be much better to have some phrase.

Yours,

JUNE 1, 1928

Dear Ring:

Here is our check in payment for the amount called for by the last royalty report.

28. Probably "Mr. Frisbie," in the June 1928 COSMOPOLITAN.

I am putting the stories in hand now, and if you want to arrange the order differently, that can be done in the galleys. Our idea is to put out the book without any suggestion of burlesque on the wrap. Will you do a preface?

Yours,

In the spring of 1928 Lardner and Grantland Rice bought tracts of land in East Hampton, about sixty miles east of Great Neck, where they built neighboring houses fronting on the ocean. It was an attempt on Lardner's part to remove himself from the excessive social demands of Great Neck. At East Hampton his circle of close friends included, besides the Rices, the John Wheelers, the James Prestons, and the Percy Hammonds.

EAST HAMPTON, LONG ISLAND.
JUNE 3.

Dear Max:-

Sure I'll do a preface if you don't want it too soon. I am still trying to think of a title. I believe the traffic policeman story,[29] which people seem to think is the best, ought to have a good position.

29. "There Are Smiles"

Dear Ring:

I have just got back from a month's vacation which was unavoidable. I have been looking over the proof of the stories, and Wheelock[30] has told me that it would be impossible to get any of the three other stories into a book published this fall. What would you think of postponing publication then, until February? The present length of the book is just about 300 pages, which is not long. Three more stories (possibly more) would bring it up to 350, which would be a full book. This would also give more time to find a really good title, and I rather think it would be advantageous in every way. So if you approve, we shall put the book over, and add the other stories.

I found on my desk a very cheerful letter from Scott. He has evidently got his book the way he wants it at last.[31]

Ever yours,

The three stories to which Perkins refers were "Ex Parte," "Insomnia," and "Old Folks' Christmas," which could not at that time be published in the projected book because they had not yet appeared in *Cosmopolitan.* Eventually "Ex Parte" came out in the November 1928 issue and "Old Folks' Christmas" in January 1929. "Insomnia," a biographically interesting but rather mediocre story, did not appear in *Round Up* and was not published in *Cosmopolitan* until May 1931.

30. John Hall Wheelock was also an editor at Scribner's. He succeeded Perkins as editor-in-chief after Perkins's death in 1947.

31. Fitzgerald's optimism was misleading. Work on the novel he had begun three years earlier, now tentatively titled "The Boy Who Killed His Mother," was not going well.

Dear Ring:

I am sending you your royalty report. I wish we had not had to put the new book off, but it was the right thing to do, and I have got several of the later stories. Did you ever write any more of those little burlesque plays? I thought if there were a number of them, we might use them in this book in some way.

Ever yours,

Sept. 28, 1928

Dear Ring:

I meant to write you to tell you how much I enjoyed "Elma".[32] I hope the play will go big, and if it shows signs of doing so, I think you ought to have it published. That will help the production, and though the sale would presumably not be large, it ought to be worthwhile even in that respect.

Scott sails tomorrow.[33] Many thanks for the tickets.

Ever yours,

32. ELMER THE GREAT.

33. The Fitzgeralds were returning home, after a disastrous summer of dissipation and disagreements in Paris.

Nov. 3, 1928

Dear Ring:

Here is a list of the stories for the book,- "And Other Stories" as we now call it. We have got a good jacket under way, but we have not put the title on because that may be changed. The upper list of titles is of those, as you will see, that have been set up. The list of four titles is of those which have not been set up. Tell us anything you want us to do about these stories, but tell us soon. We have a good large number of stories in this volume, and we do not want to reduce it any more than we ought to.

After you left the other day I almost thought you might have been speaking jokingly about the idea that anybody could think that you were "influenced" by the books you name. I do not believe you were, but certainly you might have been, because there is no question but that all these people were influenced by you. Every one of them. And I wish there were something I could do to compel you to write that 40,000 word story, or novel, or whatever it ought to be called. I do not know of any publishing news that would be more interesting than that such a book by you was to come out.

Yours always,

No record of this conversation exists, but it is interesting to note that in a 1917 *New York Times* interview, Lardner, perhaps with tongue-in-cheek, rated George Ade a greater humorist than Mark Twain, in the sense that Ade's characters were contemporary, while Twain's were not: "I never saw one of Mark Twain's characters, while I feel that I know every one about whom George Ade writes. You see, I didn't travel along the Mississippi in Mark Twain's youth, so I don't know his people. Harry Leon Wilson is a great humorist, and Finley Peter Dunne is another. But I'll bet Finley Peter Dunne is sick of writing in Irish dialect." In any case Lardner's work has its unmistakeable niche in the traditions of American humor, dating back to Twain, but with less local color and perhaps a stronger satiric strain than one finds in·Twain's major work. A major difference also is that some of Twain's characters do learn, grow, and change, whereas Lardner's characters remain, for the most part, static. Twain, therefore, comes closer to affirming the dignity and worth of life, while Lardner tends more simply to pound home the point that people are, for all their humor, too ugly or stupid to learn. There is no affirmation in Lardner's fictional world, except, implicitly, through his depiction of the dark side of humanity, a converse idealization of honesty and kindness. But even these ethical ideals are an affirmation without faith, for these virtues, when they do appear in his fictional world, go unrewarded. It is probably easier to relate Lardner's characters to Sinclair Lewis's Babbitt or to Swift's Lilliputians.

It is also significant that Perkins should stress Lardner's influence on other writers, for one could argue that no other twentieth-century American writer, except perhaps Hemingway, has been so widely imitated, primarily for his accurate rendering of American dialogue. One writer, Arthur Kober, spoke for many in 1951: "It was a baseball writer . . . who had the greatest influence on me. Ring Lardner. There is a man who had a wonderful ear for speech. His preoccupation with phonetics, his ability to record speech as he heard it, the manners and mores of the people—he had it all." And both James T. Farrell and Ernest Hemingway have acknowledged their early efforts to imitate the style particularly of Lardner's *Chicago Tribune* "In the Wake of the News" column.

12 EAST 86TH STREET
NEW YORK CITY
NOVEMBER 6.

Dear Max:-

I have added "The High Rollers" to the list of possible stories for the book. Cosmopolitan has had it about two weeks. It is not anything to boast of, but I think it is better than some of the others— "The Spinning Wheel", for one. Harper's Bazar is going to run another one that is not on the list. The title is "Contract." Are you sure "I Can't Breathe" wasn't in "The Love Nest"? It seems to me I wrote it a long time ago.

I am marking with an X the stories I am not keen about and which I think the book might get along without.

"I Can't Breathe" had been published in the September 1926 *Cosmopolitan*. One of Lardner's better stories, it is the often-anthologized diary of a young female flirt who records her "breathless" romances with four indistinguishable young men. The story is noteworthy primarily for its masterful rendition of adolescent hyperbole.

Lardner's list of stories does not survive, but the "X'd" stories presumably were among the ones Perkins omitted from the projected book— "The Jade Necklace," "The Spinning Wheel," "The Venomous Viper of the Volga," "Wedding Day," and "Absent Minded Beggar."

Nov. 13, 1928

Dear Ring:

I have now got "Contract" and I shall get "The High Rollers". Mr. Flaum of the Cosmopolitan, to whom I was referred there, did not know about it. I am estimating the length of the book with a view to leaving out the stories which you think not so good. Have you thought of a title? I think that "— And Other Stories" is good in one way, but it does give the impression that there is nothing new about the book, which is against it.

Ever yours,

Dear Ring:

Here is a small check,-[34] but the next one will be bigger. I guess we'll call the book, "And Other Stories". I am setting up those that we have added since last fall, but there are two that we cannot put in, "High Rollers" and "Twice Told Tales". Ray Long does not know when he will use them. I shall soon send you proofs.

I have been meaning to read the Telegraph but they do not sell any copies in my town.

Yours always,

The New York *Morning Telegraph* had hired Lardner in December 1928 to write four articles a week, on any subject he wished, at a then phenomenal salary of $50,000 a year. However, his column, titled "Ring's Side," lasted only two months, before the *Telegraph's* financial problems forced a termination of the agreement.

Dec. 27, 1928

Dear Ring:

This is to put on record with you what I said by telephone yesterday:-

The Literary Guild wishes to take for their book of the

34. Marginalia indicates the amount of the check was $297.50.

month for either April, May, or June (probably April, and almost certainly not June) a book of your stories to embrace those in "How to Write Short Stories," "The Love Nest," and those we have already in type for the book we had planned to publish this spring. They agree to pay $13,500, which we propose should be divided equally between you and ourselves.

The job is quite a big one, and we ought to get ahead immediately, and are even now making estimates on the printing so that we ought to know as soon as possible what stories you wish to omit.- But as the book is to be about 250,000 words, it would be undesirable to omit more than two or three stories anyhow. I hope you won't want to omit "The Facts" which is a light story but a very funny one, extremely well told. Another point to be considered is that the book should contain as large a proportion of the new stories as possible.

As to the general proposition, we think it highly advantageous because it will put a very fine book by you in the hands of some 70,000 people, to say nothing of those to whom we can sell copies through the regular trade. And so your public will be very greatly enlarged. It will also lead, we think, to a re-estimation of you as a writer of stories, etc., in all the reviewing papers, which would also be most advantageous.

We of course, shall scrap "And Other Stories" entirely, only using the corrected proofs to reset that part of the new book.

This is the first book we have had with the Guild because we were unwilling to sell anything to them until they gave up cutting prices. I think they will give it rather special attention, certainly a great amount of publicity and advertising,- more than a publisher could afford to give to any one book.

Ever yours,

The selection of a volume by Lardner as a Literary Guild book marked clear recognition of Lardner's literary talent. The selection committee of the Guild at that time included Carl Van Doren, Hendrik Willem Van Loon, Elinor Wylie, Joseph Wood Krutch, and Burton Rascoe. The contractual arrangements were stated in the following letter to Perkins:

The Literary Guild
of America
55 Fifth Avenue
New York
December 26, 1928.
Chas. Scribner's Sons,
597 Fifth Avenue,
New York City.
Gentlemen: *Attention of Mr. Maxwell Perkins.*
This will confirm our understanding of the purchase by the Literary Guild of an edition of Ring Lardner's Stories. These stories embrace two previous books of Ring Lardner and the third book in the course of preparation.
We agree to take an edition in a quantity sufficient for our subscribers. This will be approximately 70,000 copies.
We agree to pay for this edition the sum of thir-

teen thousand five hundred dollars ($13,500.00), the payment to be made net within sixty (60) days from publication date.

You agree to publish the book during the first ten days of April, May or June, 1929. We will advise you of the definite month of publication sixty days in advance.

We agree to use the books of our edition to send to regular Guild subscribers and in no case to sell single copies.

This book is to be completely re-set in format for a single volume embracing about 250,000 words and about 250 pages.

If your printing plant can meet the delivery date and price of our printers we will be glad to have you deliver us printed sheets from paper supplied by ourselves. Otherwise you agree to furnish us with an extra set of plates at cost.

The composition and plate cost shall not be included in figuring the cost of printing the Guild edition.

We are very anxious to cooperate with you in promoting the trade sale of this book and urge you to make use of our Publicity Department in any way which you feel will be of service to you.

If this agrees with your understanding will you be good enough to sign and return the enclosed carbon copy for our files.

Very truly yours,
THE LITERARY
GUILD OF
AMERICA,INC.,
M. J. Sutliff,
Managing Director.

JAN. 14, 1929

Mr. Ring Lardner
New Colonial Hotel
Nassau, Bahamas

Literary Guild and we wish to call your book quotes Round Up quotes with subtitle quote The Stories of Ring Lardner quote. Hope you approve. Please wire.

Maxwell Perkins

The title "Round Up" was apparently Perkins's suggestion, selected from such other titles as "Our Kind," "Some of Ours," "Such as We," and "Sorts and Conditions." Perkins anticipated the criticism that the expression was "especially western," and argued

that "it is now used about almost every
sort of gathering together,- even that
of crooks." The title is misleading, but
its cowboy connotations probably did
enhance the sales of the book.

NASSAU
1929 FEB 9 PM 11 27

MAXWELL PERKINS=
    CHARLES SCRIBNERS SONS FIFTH AVE NEW-
YORK (NY)= I PREFER ENSEMBLE TO ROUND UP
DONT YOU.

RING LARDNER.

FEB. 14, 1929

Dear Ring:

    I must tell you that we were committed to the title
"Round Up" before your telegram came. I am sorry this was
so. We did not want to take a title you did not fully approve,
and I was stupid about your visit to Nassau. I see that you
did not leave nearly as soon as I thought, and then I myself
had to go down to Key West, and in the meantime everything went forward here, and the title page and cover and
wrap, and everything else was made. I do think though, that
we got a good title. We suggested a half dozen to the Literary
Guild and they instantly and enthusiastically picked out

"Round Up". We thought it a truly American phrase which is applied to any kind of a gathering together nowadays, well-sounding, and extremely effective typographically. We ourselves are publishing 20,000 of the book which makes a complete printing of about 90,000 and so large an edition made it necessary for us to hurry everything. I would have cabled you again though if I had not had to go away. I am sorry. I hope you won't much mind.

Ever yours,

Feb. 28, 1929

Dear Ring:

Here is the royalty report for the sales of your books in the last six months.- But the next report will show something really substantial.

We are thinking of making up a little collection of short stories containing one by each of the following writers and yourself: Thomas Boyd, Struthers Burt, Conrad Aiken, Scott Fitzgerald, Stark Young, Morley Callaghan, and Ernest Hemingway. We could pay only 2¢ royalty, but that is a cent and a half more than was proposed by the Modern Library which wanted to get out a volume containing most of these writers — it was their proposal that suggested this one really, because almost all the writers in the book they planned were those for whom we published. If this works out, and you will let a story of yours go in, I would choose "Some Like Them Cold". I always thought it was an almost perfect story, and yet it has never been played up to the extent that "A Golden Honeymoon" or "Champion" have, for instance. Besides, such a book as this might have some educational sales in colleges, and I think this story would be the most suitable in some ways for that audience.

Ever yours,

Dear Ring:

I enclose a check for three thousand. This is not quite all of the balance, but I thought you might want it instantly, and have done it without looking up the matter.

Please come in when you can.

Yours always,

MARCH 12, 1929

Dear Ring:

We naturally want to cooperate to the limit with the Literary Guild in the exploitation of your book. Will you help by giving us a list of the reporters and special writers on New York newspapers known to you?[35]

And will you be interviewed? If so, and you really should, the Guild will arrange the whole thing, and in a very convenient way. Also will you supply photos of yourself and family?

35. This request and the others in this letter had been made of Perkins by Selma Robinson, who handled publicity for the Literary Guild.

We have certainly got a grand chance now with all these stories in one volume, even apart from the Guild, and we ought to do every conceivable thing to make the most of it.- So let me know.

Ever yours,

MARCH 19, 1929

Dear Ring:

I am sending you six copies of the book, as usual;- and I shall let you have any news about sales, or anything of importance, whenever there is any.

Hoping you do not find the publicity part of the business too trying, and that you will go through with it, I am,

Ever yours,

MARCH 20, 1929

Dear Ring:

I thought I would let you know that we discussed advertising plans on your book today, and that we are going to spend, within a few weeks after publication, all of our share from the Literary Guild deal. We shall have several full pages in the Times Supplement,the first to appear two weeks after the book does,- in order to gain the support of the seventy thousand or so Guild readers. We have never thought that you have had the sale your books are entitled to, and we are going to try to get it now, and to build for the future. Of course you never can tell, but I wanted you to know that we were going to make the most of the opportunity.

Ever yours,

MARCH 29, 1929

Dear Ring:

I am sending you a copy of the Guild edition of the book which is, of course, from the same plates as ours and so does not differ internally,- only on the wrap and the cover,- which I think they made a bad job of.

Aren't you doing that 40,000 word story you were telling me about?

Ever yours,

APRIL 5, 1929

Dear Ring:

I hope things are all right with you now. I wish you would come in here sometime when you pass by. In Sunday's Times there is a very long, and intentionally very fine review, and I have just heard from the Tribune that Lewis Mumford is to review the book for them, probably in the April 14th issue — Spring book number.

Always yours,

Perkins's reference is to a prolonged drinking bout Lardner had experienced. "George [Kaufman] and I worked on the play [*June Moon*] nearly all last spring and summer," Lardner wrote to Fitzgerald in February 1930, "and when the New York opening was over, I went on a bat that lasted nearly three months and haven't been able to work since, so it's a good thing that the play paid dividends." Apparently Mrs. Lardner had informed Perkins of the problem, for on 2 April he had sent Lardner's latest royalties, a check for $750, to Mrs. Lardner. This illness proved to be the beginning of a rather bad time for Lardner; he spent much of 1930 in hospitals, not only for treatment of tuberculosis but also for a heart problem.

Critical appraisals of the thirty-five stories in *Round Up* exhibited nothing new in the valuation of Lardner's work. All the reviews were essentially positive, though some reviewers perceived that the newer stories, though effective, did not quite match the artistry of the older ones. The *Times* review, by John Chamberlain, typically acknowledged Lardner's achievement: " 'Round Up' gives the full measure of his talent—a talent that is mature and sure-footed." Lewis Mumford's review in the *Herald Tribune* was more restrained, but he admitted that "the short stories brought together in 'Round Up' must be counted among the few that will be readable twenty years hence."

Dear Ring:

I am enclosing herewith the first of a series of advertisements to appear in the Times Book Review,- this one on April 21st.

Ever yours,

MAY 31, 1929

Dear Ring:

I enclose a small check. The next one will be very considerably better. "Round Up" has sold in our edition now just about 10,000 copies. We have every right to hope the sale will go on. It has been a very sure and steady one since the start.

If only you would do that 40,000 word story you thought of, now would be the time for it, with the great distribution of "Round Up" as a background.

Ever yours,

JUNE 14, 1929

Dear Ring:

What have you ever done about movie rights to your stories? A agent named Bennett, well thought of, took a copy of "Round Up" in the idea of talking to some producer about it, and I thought it was all right that he should see whether he could get an offer. The talkie element seems to me to add greatly to the possibilities of what you have written. I have a fear though, that you yourself may have made arrangements which would nullify any results that this man might get.- The movie rights are, of course, wholly yours. We should not expect to share in them at all, unless we ourselves made an actual sale, in which case we would only take an agent's commission of 10%. I wish you would tell me though, how the matter stands, because I think. there may well be a demand for your stories in view of the change in character of movies. "Round Up" goes on quite steadily though not rapidly.

Have you ever begun on the long story? And do you ever hear anything about Scott? What I hear is not good.

Ever yours,

Perkins assumed, reasonably enough, that the believable dialogue of Lardner's stories would be most attractive to the movie industry newly embarked at this time on the production of movies with sound tracks.

News of the Fitzgeralds was indeed disturbing. In the spring of 1929, after the lease on Ellerslie had expired, they had gone again to Europe. But Zelda's concentration on her dancing was greater than ever, and Fitzgerald, who had written Perkins that he was working on his novel from a "new angle," had actually dropped the matricide story in favor of a new novel, the forerunner of *Tender Is the Night,*

which he called "The Drunkard's Holiday." In the insecurity of his marital
and literary status, he had also become
jealous of Hemingway and had quar-
reled with him over a number of trifles.

EAST HAMPTON, LONG ISLAND
JUNE 19, 1929.

Dear Max:-

I had a letter from Mr. Bennet, whom (it seems) I met
in Waco, Texas, years ago. He said he hadn't been able to
peddle any of the "Round Up" stories to the talkie people. I
am not tied up for movie rights and would be glad if Scribner's could sell some of the stories.

"Show business" has kept me so busy that I haven't
even considered the novelette.[36] But show business is slow on
financial returns and maybe I'll be asking you for some
advance soon.

I haven't heard a word of Scott. Hasn't he ever finished
the novel?

Sincerely,

JUNE 20, 1929

Dear Ring:

Scott has not finished his novel, and I have only had
one letter from him. In that he mentioned it as if he did not

36. During much of 1929 Lardner worked diligently on JUNE MOON, in
collaboration with George Kaufman.

like to talk about it, and I get very bad reports of him,-
although they are not direct and may be more or less un-
founded. I am afraid he is in a nervous and dejected condition. Couldn't you write him a letter? Letters are not much
help, but one from you would help him more than one from
anyone else. If only he does not blow up in some way, he will
come out all right in the end, but I think he is pretty hard
pressed with worries and disappointments.

I should say now that the sale on "Round Up"
amounted to a little beyond 11,000, and it goes on well. I
think we could give you the royalty on that whenever you
needed it.

Ever yours,

JULY 2, 1929

Dear Ring:

I am sending you a check for two thousand dollars,
charging it against your royalty. The total amount earned to
date in royalties is $4441.64, and if you wish, I can send you
the remainder. But if the $2,000 will serve your present pur-
poses, I thought it would be better to send only that. Don't
hesitate to ask for the rest if you want it.

I am mighty glad you are writing to Scott.

Always yours,

SEPT. 19, 1929

Dear Ring:

I am sending you the royalty report on the sales in the
six months preceding August first, including the sale of

"Round Up". The amount earned accordingly, a little short of $3,000 over the payments we have made you, is not actually due until December, but you know you can always call upon us. I wish you would also do so in person sometime.

Ever yours,

OCTOBER 11, 1929

Dear Ring:

I am delighted with the reviews of your play. Don't you think we ought to publish it?— if it's to be the success it looks like, we should for there should be sufficient sale, at least.

I have much better news about Scott. He is getting on well.

Ever yours,

June Moon is a moderately good three-act play, based on "Some Like Them Cold," which had considerable success, running for 273 performances in New York. Critical response was favorable, and the play was included in Burns Mantle's *Best Plays of 1929-30.* Two of the songs from the play, "June Moon" and "Montana Moon," were published separately and achieved some popularity.

During much of September 1929 Fitzgerald was working hard on his new novel and momentarily regained much of his old enthusiasm. His concentration was such, in fact, that his obvious study of his friend Gerald Murphy, on whom the hero of the novel was in part based, strained the friendship with the Murphys.

Oct. 21, 1929

Dear Ring:

I am sending you herewith the check for the balance earned in royalties.

As for "June Moon", if it comes to us soon enough so that we can get it out during November, I think we ought to do it and take advantage of the play's novelty.

I hope you are getting over the cold. I could tell you a sure cure, but I know you would be bored to hear it.

Ever yours,

In 1929, Lardner's royalties from Scribner's were paid as follows: on 3 January, $3000; on 4 March, $3000; on 2 April, $750; on 1 June, $203.27; on 1 July, $2000; and 21 October, $2919.94; for a yearly total of $11,873.21.

DEC. 11, 1929

Dear Ring:

I hope you won't mind my reminding you about "June Moon". I suppose the delay can't be helped, but the less of it there is, the greater the sale,- and we will do very speedy work in getting it out as soon as we have it in our hands.

Ever yours,

THE CROYDON
12 EAST 86TH STREET
NEW YORK CITY
DECEMBER 31, 1929.

Dear Max:-

George Kaufman is trying to get a script into shape for publication, but it is such a mess now that it may take a little time.

Have you seen Scott since he came back, or is he back? I haven't heard a word from him.

Sincerely,

The collaboration with George Kaufman was a compatible one. Lardner wrote most of the play, with Kaufman suggesting revision and providing a sense of dramatic structure in which

Lardner's characters could best reveal
themselves. Kaufman understood
Lardner's humor and satire, and
worked hard to enhance it in dramatic
form.

Jan. 2, 1930

Dear Ring:

Thanks for your note. I wish George Kaufman would
hurry up, but I dare say it is a hard piece of work. Shall I
make up a contract distributing the royalty equally, or how?

Scott is still in Paris, but I hear from himself, and from
Hemingway, that he is doing well now, and that he sees a
clear road ahead for the novel. The fact is that he evidently
struck a knot in it that he could not untie for a long time, but
now has.

Won't you come to lunch some day soon,- or at least
stop in here? I want to speak to you about one plan we have,
and other things.

Fitzgerald does not appear to
have informed Perkins that he had put
aside the old matricide novel to work
on "The Drunkard's Holiday."

FEB. 14, 1930

Dear Ring:

I am sending you the contract in three copies. I did not ask you about the terms and it is true that 7 1/2% is mighty little, but with a play which would not sell, at best, more than a few thousands of copies, it is truly impossible to pay a higher royalty without loss to the publisher. If you think the contract is all right, and will sign and return it, I shall send it also to Mr. Kaufman.

Ever yours,

FEB. 24, 1930

Dear Ring:

I am sending back your copy of the contract which has been signed also by George Kaufmann- And I am also sending separately, the first of the galley proof. I hope you can read this so that we may avoid sending it to Mr. Kaufmann, and get on faster. The rest of the proof will follow right away.

Always yours,

MARCH 13, 1930

Dear Ring:

I am sending you a royalty report which shows that there will be due you on the first of June, $693.35. I hope you may soon have enough stories or material of some kind to make another book. "Round Up" went into the hands of about 100,000 people, and it should have enlarged your book public. It was that we hoped it would do and when we put out another volume, we shall see if we have succeeded.

Ever yours,

Dear Ring:

I hope everything is going well with you. I am enclosing herewith a check for the amount due you according to the last royalty report.

Don't you think you could have another book to be published about a year from now? Even now there ought to be quite a number of stories ready, but the fiction marked is so frightfully upset and depressed that I would think it was better not to hurry.

Ever yours,

Sept. 11, 1930

Dear Ring:

Herewith is your royalty report. I do not suppose you will want the check until December, but if you do, I think we should be very glad to send it.

Always yours,

Dear Ring:

Here is the check you speak of. I wish it were larger. As for the O'Brien letter, we shall write giving consent.[37] The publication is to be confined to England.

Things have been very bad with Scott on account of Zelda, but now they seem very much better.

Always yours,

At Paris on 23 April 1930, Zelda had suffered a mental breakdown. Flamboyant as she was, Zelda had always felt subordinate to Fitzgerald's personality and reputation; Fitzgerald had drawn freely from his life with Zelda for the subject matter of his fiction. Her obsession with ballet dancing can be seen as a tardy and desperate attempt to assert her own character in the turbulent marriage. After her breakdown there were frequent hallucinations concerning Fitzgerald which seem to exhibit her jealousy and resentment over his dominant role in the marriage.

37. Edward J. O'Brien annually published a volume of the year's best short stories. The letter refers to a request to use "The Golden Honeymoon" in a volume entitled MODERN AMERICAN SHORT STORIES, published in London in 1932.

Dear Ring:

Do you think you would have enough stories to make a volume by next fall? I think if you have, we ought not to let them await publication in book form any longer. On the whole, "Round Up" got a pretty wide distribution, and undoubtedly put your stories into the hands of a great many people who had never read them between book covers before.- And so we might find that for a new collection we should have a wider public. As a matter of fact, we should not have to put a collection for fall publication in hand for some four months, and by that time you might have a number of short stories published. But if you think well of the plan, and will tell me which stories are available and where they have been published or will be published, I can manage to get them together.

Always yours,

THE VANDERBILT HOTEL
THIRTY-FOURTH STREET EAST AT PARK AVENUE
NEW YORK
FEBRUARY 13, 1931.

Dear Max:-

My health hasn't been so good - I guess I am paying for my past - and I'm not averaging more than four short stories a year. None of the recent ones has been anything to boast of and I'm afraid there won't be enough decent ones to print by fall. Maybe I'll get more energetic or inspired or something in the next few months.

This is just a temporary address. you can always reach me in care of the Bell Syndicate, 63 Park Row.

Sincerely,

Lardner frequently stayed at a hotel in New York, to work, rest, or recuperate from the illnesses of later years. Sometimes he stayed away from home for several days. Existing letters to his family make clear his devotion, but he also craved the social life of New York restaurants, clubs, and theaters. He was a frequent inhabitant particularly of the Friars' Club, the Lambs Club, and the Algonquin.

FEB. 16, 1931

Dear Ring:

I am sorry you have not been feeling well.- But spring is not so far off now, and that always, I find, brings a man up a good many notches. I wish you would take a year off from New York, and the theatre, etc., and quietly do a novel!

Always yours,

Dear Ring:

I am sending you the royalty report due February first, and a check for the royalties. I wish it were larger,- and I hope before long you will be able to let us bring out another book.

Ever yours,

Dear Ring:

I have received a letter from Paul de H. Reed, Director of Radio for the United Advertising Agency, Inc. He wants to arrange to put "You Know Me Al" on the radio, and he hopes to make something as successful as Amos and Andy. He wants to pay us a small fee for the right to do it, but so far as you are concerned, he would pay something like a royalty which might amount to a great deal, and particularly if you would be willing to undertake to make the "script". He spoke of as much as several hundred a week as not beyond the possibilities. It does seem as if there were great possibilities in "You Know Me Al" from a radio standpoint, and I hope you will consider the question of doing them a script. It would not be so very difficult. Will you let me know as soon as you can how you feel about the proposition so that if you are favorable, we can get the thing under way?

I heard that one of your boys had a bad fall up in Andover, but since there was nothing in the papers about it, I hoped it was not very serious in the end.

Always yours,

Lardner was hardly up to writing
a script at this time, and the proposition apparently died of neglect.

The "bad fall" was Ring, Jr.'s,
then fourteen and attending Andover,
who had slipped from the fourth floor
of a dormitory while attempting to
crawl from one window to another and
had fractured his pelvis and shoulder.

MAY 5, 1931

Dear Ring:

I hope you are all right, or at any rate that you soon
will be now that spring is here. I am enclosing a copy of a
letter[38] I wrote you some time ago, because it may never have
reached you, having presumably been forwarded to Arizona.
I think there might be a good deal of money in this for you,
and I called up your brother at the Bell Syndicate today
when this Mr. Reed, of the letter, called me up to say that he
was very anxious to get on with the matter.

Always yours,

On the advice of his doctors,
Lardner had spent most of March and
April 1931 at the Desert Sanatorium in
Tucson, in an attempt to better his
tubercular condition.

38. The preceding letter of 30 April 1931.

Perkins's sympathy in the following letter results from his learning of another of Lardner's stays in the hospital, which were more extensive and more frequent by this time. This particular hospitalization was for about a month, after which Lardner moved into an apartment on East End, where he, Ellis, and two of the boys, David and John, spent the winter. David was then only twelve, and John, nineteen, was a reporter for the *Herald Tribune*. The other two boys were away at school: James, at Harvard, and Ring, Jr., at Andover.

SEPT. 2, 1931

Dear Ring:

I am terribly sorry you are laid up, and I hope you are not finding it too unpleasant.

I am enclosing a royalty report, but it does not call for a great deal of money, I am sorry to say.

Scott is soon to be here, and with Zelda who is well again.

I have tried to think of some book to send you but there doesn't seem to be any. If there is anything you want, do let me know.

Always yours,

The royalty due was $208.93, which Mrs. Lardner, as acting head of the family during Lardner's illness, requested immediately instead of as usual in December. Lardner had been unable to work for five months, and the family needed the money. In a subsequent note of thanks, Mrs. Lardner commented: "Ring is not much better and is still unable to do any work. I am rather discouraged about him because he worries so over not being able to work that the rest he is having does not do him the good it should." She went on to say: "I have been so sorry about Zelda and do hope they are still getting along all right. Do you suppose there is anyone left in the world who is well physically, mentally *and financially?*"

Perkins was overly optimistic about Zelda, though she had improved sufficiently to be released from Montreux in the spring of 1931 and to come home to America with Fitzgerald in September.

The lapse of nearly a year in the correspondence at this point suggests again the extent to which Lardner's deteriorating physical condition had prevented him from working. Moreover, the following letter itself hints of self-doubt and depression in a way Lardner had not previously exhibited.

Dear Max:-

Early in the summer, one of the Post's associate editors wrote me such a tactless letter, suggesting that the new series of baseball letters be brought to a conclusion in two more installments that I, then in a low mental condition, thought the whole series must be pretty bad though I had felt quite proud of part of it when I had sent it in. His words were chosen with a view, I guess, to lessening the shock of the premature conclusion, whereas if he had written frankly, saying that the Post could no longer afford to pay the very liberal price it had set on the series, I would have understood perfectly and thought little of it. For a time I banished the idea of offering the series to you for a book, but later on I reread some of the acceptance letters from Lorimer and other Post editors, as well as a bunch of nice "fan mail," and got steamed up about it again. I honestly don't know how the present interest in baseball compares with the past, but I presume that Brooklyn's recent spurt (the "hero" is a Brooklyn player) ought to be a help. Please read the whole thing when you feel strong and healthy and tell me what you think. I enclose the final installment, which should be published in a week or so. If Brooklyn wins the pennant, a book appearing simultaneously with the world's series might go.

In the spring of 1932 Lardner had written six new "busher" baseball stories obviously imitative of the Jack Keefe letters. They consist of letters from rookie Brooklyn outfielder Danny Warner to his girl friend Jessie and her responses. The six stories were published serially in the *Saturday Evening Post* and then in book form by Scribner's under the title *Lose with a Smile* in 1933. Though the book is a pale version of *You Know Me Al*, it exhibits all Lardner's mastery of the "busher" dialect and the epistolary form and is a remarkable effort by a man in extremely ill health and unable to write for any sustained length of time.

AUG. 17, 1932

Dear Ring:

I am sending you your regular royalty report. The payment is due on December first, but I daresay we could manage to make it sooner if you wanted it, although it is not for a very large sum.

I had always supposed that we would publish your Saturday Evening Post baseball articles in early 1933, but because of all the things I have had to do lately, I only read one, the early one. I am getting all there are, and probably now the last one has been published. I thought your radio pieces in the New Yorker were extremely good, and read all of them in the idea that they might make a book, but I hardly think so because they deal with such transitory matters.

I am sending you a book I think you would like, but don't read it if you do not.[39]

Scott's address which is complicated, is: La Paix, Rodger's Forge, Maryland. He did not look so very well, but he seemed in great spirits, and Zelda is getting on. She is not as

39. Amusingly, Scribner's intended to send Lardner a copy of THE STREAM OF TIME but sent by mistake STUDIES IN NAPOLEONIC WARS.

pretty as she was, but I really liked her better,- though I always did like her. Did I tell you that we are publishing a novel by her?

Always yours,

The royalty due was $222.73. Sales records also indicate that, in 1932, 20,366 copies of *How To Write Short Stories* had been sold; 8,633 copies of *What of It?*; 12,904 copies of *The Love Nest;* 6,764 copies of *the Story of a Wonder Man*; and 15,261 copies of *Round Up* (in addition to the 70,000 copies of *Round Up* sold through the Literary Guild).

The "radio pieces" are a series of critical columns Lardner wrote for *The New Yorker* in 1932 and 1933 on the standards of radio entertainment. It is a curious sort of crusade by a dying man against illiteracy, bad taste, and off-color songs on the radio programs to which Lardner listened from his hospital bed. The high point of his articles is his parodies of Cole Porter's "Night and Day": "Night and day under the fleece of me/There's an Oh, such a flaming furneth burneth the grease of me . . . . Night and day under my dermis, dear,/There's a spot just as hot as coffee kept in a thermos, dear . . . ."

Perkins's news of the Fitzgeralds was guarded. In January, following her

father's death, Zelda had experienced
a second breakdown, and Fitzgerald
had taken her to Baltimore for treatment, eventually leasing a house called
La Paix nearby. Zelda improved sufficiently to live there quietly during
much of 1932 and 1933, and Fitzgerald
began again to work consistently on
Tender Is the Night, a drastic "replan-
ning" of the projected 1929 novel "The
Drunkard's Holiday." Zelda's novel,
Save Me the Waltz, is a strikingly autobiographical work written in about
six weeks time during her confinement
in the Baltimore hospital. Like her earlier study of ballet, the novel appears
most obviously to be an attempt to
compete with Fitzgerald for success
and popularity. Fitzgerald was angry
at the directness with which she had
drawn from their own lives, though he
had done much the same in many of
his own narratives. But he and Perkins
worked hard to edit the novel for publication.

THURSDAY, AUGUST 18.

Dear Max:-

A check for that $222.73 early next week would be a
life-saver; or rather, a life insurance saver. However, if it isn't
convenient I can manage to get over the hurdle in some other
way.[40]

I mailed you the proof of the final Post installment

40. As a result of his illness Lardner's income was drastically reduced in
1932, and he was finding himself in need of money.

yesterday or the day before. It hasn't been published yet, but certainly ought to be within three weeks. You are right about the New Yorker stuff - It is much too topical and local for publication in a book.

I am very much steamed up over the news of Zelda's novel and hope you will keep me posted on the date of publication, etc.

Sincerely,

AUG. 23, 1932

Dear Ring:

Here is the check. I meant to get it off sooner, but the Cashier's Department never gets very excited nowadays[41] about paying out money. I hope it gets there in time to save the life insurance.

I have been reading the baseball stories with very great enjoyment myself. I shall write you about them very soon.

Always yours,

SEPT. 8, 1932.

Dear Ring:

Would you let us publish the baseball series on the basis of a 10% royalty on the first five thousand? I am sorry I was so long in writing you about the letters but these days are such bad days we have to look into things closely and plan about them. I think the material is very good indeed, and in

41. Perkins is alluding to the Depression, and to the hard times resulting from it for the book trade.

some ways better than "You Know Me, Al" although I don't know that it is as popular. It has much more subtility, many more implications, it seems to me. We would publish it at $2.00 and we'd rather hope to use some of the illustrations if you thought well of them. We'd try to give it a rather special look, somewhat larger than the other books.- And a title which seems to us very good would be "Lose With A Smile". We took up the question with the American News Company on the idea of making it an inexpensive book. They thought *they* would do as well with a $2.00 book, but they did not regard the material as being for the lower grade public, and neither do I,- rather the other way.

They agreed with us that we ought not to publish it by any means until early in 1933. All the advantages of early selling which began last May for Fall books would be lost if it should be put out now. All the book stores have invested their money in stock and hate to take anything else, however good. But if published early next Spring it would get a lot of attention and the prospects would be excellent, particularly if business has by then really improved, which it has not yet.

I had a letter from Zelda (I'll soon send you her novel) in which she said that Scott had got the way clear and was working on his novel![42]

I am sending you Hemingway's book[43] and I believe you will like it a lot.

Always yours,

---

42. TENDER IS THE NIGHT was finally published in 1934.
43. DEATH IN THE AFTERNOON.

MAX PERKINS,CARE CHARLES SCRIBNERS SONS =
597 FIFTH AVE NEWYORK NY =
ARRANGEMENT YOU SUGGEST IS ALL RIGHT EX-
CEPT THAT I DO NOT WANT THOSE ILLUSTRA-
TIONS PRESENT ADDRESS IS EASTHAMPTON NO
LONGER HAVE THE APARTMENT AT TWENTY
FIVE EAST END DID YOU SEND HEMMINGWAY
BOOK THERE =
RING LARDNER.

SEPT. 17, 1932

Dear Ring:

I didn't like the pictures either.- The trade department
though thought they would help, but of course we shan't use
them. I'll send a contract.

The Hemingway did come back — it was mis-ad-
dressed because it was vacation season and the work was
done by one unused to it — but we sent it right out to you at
Easthampton. I'm sending Zelda's book.

Yours,

SEPT. 21, 1932

Dear Ring:

Here is the contract. You don't object to our doing
some sort of decorative illustration, do you? We want to

break the text somehow. The letters come one right after another, and some relief to the eye seems desirable.

Always yours,

Dear Ring:

You may have been surprised to get another copy of "Death in the Afternoon" but I daresay you will discover that it is one Ernest sent you and inscribed. The reason it came so late was that he has been away off in the mountains of Montana hunting, and the copies waited a long time before he got back to sign them.

Your manuscript is with the printer, and I hope we shall have proof soon.

Ever yours,

Nov. 15, 1932

Dear Ring:

I am sending you herewith some samples of the work of the illustrator Gene McNerney. It seems to us very desirable, if he can do it to suit you, that we should have some little decorative illustrations to break up the monotony of type in "Lose with a Smile". The book is very small, and it would be more marketable if it could be given a somewhat higher price which decorative illustrations would warrant.

Let us know what you think.

Always yours,

FEB. 1, 1933

Dear Ring:

I am sending you herewith a check for *three* hundred dollars.[44] We have to figure awfully close. I thought if we sent you this now and published the book in March, we might later be able to send you a couple of hundred more. We should be willing to keep up with the sale, but we cannot tell yet what that is going to be at all. Booksellers won't order anything to speak of in advance. A large part of our business now has to be done on a consigment basis. I shall watch the sale, and the moment the book has earned more than three hundred, which might even be by the time it was published, we could send more if you want it. I hope this will seem all right. The worst of it is I know you will say it does, even if it doesn't.

Ever yours,

Royalty payments to Lardner in his last years amounted to $1,109.77 in 1930, $356.35 in 1931, $363.48 in 1932, and $300 in 1933.

The varying tone of the following letter is significant. The depression over his ill health and declining creative powers is evident, but so is Lardner's ability to retain his sense of humor.

44. Lardner had requested an advance in royalties of $500 on the sales of LOSE WITH A SMILE.

Dear Max:-

Some day I will probably realize that there is a depression. I wouldn't have asked you for any advance if I hadn't got into a sudden jam. The doctor and I decided that my place was the desert for a while, and not having done any real work since June, I was obliged to borrow money. I borrowed less than I needed, figuring I would sell a story to the Post. Once I wrote a complete story, "Alibi Ike," between 2 P.M. and midnight, with an hour off for dinner. This last one was begun in July and finished ten days ago, and the Post turned it down just as promptly as it had accepted "Ike." Since then, Bill Lengel has said it was great (but he ain't the boss), Collier's has rejected it as too long and tenuous (It runs 7,500 words) and Mencken has told me it was too much of a domestica symphonica or something for the Mercury. Mr. Graeve (Delineator), suggested, perhaps sarcastically, by Mencken, now has it as a week-end guest and I have asked him to return it to my brother on the Times, who will give it to some poor author's agent to peddle. I have always scoffed at agents, but I am leaving tomorrow morning for La Quinta, California, to be gone till the money has disappeared. I have promised the doctor that I won't work on anything but a play which George Kaufman has been waiting for me to start for three years; of course, I will have to cheat a little, but I can't cheat much.

What I started to say is that the fiction story (really not bad, and just as really not a Pulitzer prize winner) has a great many local stops to make, and if I were to stay here and wait till the last possible purchaser had said no, I would die of jitters. Your loan has made it possible for me to get out of here before I am committed to Bellevue, and I am truly grateful. I won't need the "other" two hundred, and if the sale of "Lose With a Smile" never totals the amount you have advanced me, I will see to it that you don't lose. The agent can make the rounds much quicker than I could from 3,500 miles away.

This letter doesn't seem to be properly constructed or quite clear. That is a symptom of my state of mind, but the fact that I can laugh at the succession of turn-downs of a story which everybody but the Post has had a kind word for but no inclination to buy, makes me hopeful for the future. Maybe some day I can write a piece about the story's Cook's Tour - it is the first one I ever wrote that wasn't accepted by the first or second publication to which it was offered, and that either means go west old man or quit writing fiction or both.

Thanks again, and honestly I want you to forget the "balance" because I can easily get along without it.

Will you send me a couple of copies of "Lose With a Smile" when it is published?

Yours,

The widely traveled story was "Poodle." Perkins wrote immediately to Lardner's brother Rex, requesting a chance to publish it in *Scribner's Magazine,* but it had already been accepted by *Delineator* where it appeared in the January 1934 issue.

On the same day of the above letter, Lardner wrote to his sister Lena in Niles, Michigan:
"The doctors think it is necessary for me to get out of this climate and into

the desert. So Ellis and I are leaving
next Saturday by boat, via the Panama
Canal, for California (on borrowed
money) and will stay for three
months . . . , hoping my condition
will improve enough to permit me to
work again. It is hard to leave John
and not to see the other boys occasionally, but I think it will be best in the
long run."

He did work on the play he had
mentioned, completing one act, with
fragments of a second, before he died.
Interestingly, it was to deal with rigid
bourgeois moral attitudes toward alco-
holism. The protagonist is an alco-
holic.

JULY 28, 1933.

Dear Ring:

I've read all your "Over The Waves" again. I do think
that they are extremely good;-that you never did anything of
that sort any better. But it does seem to me that as a book,
business being what it now is, it would not be likely to sell,
and if so it would harm the trade. It is superficially very, very
contemporary, and I think too much so to make a successful
book.

Always yours,

At the age of 48, Ring Lardner
died of a heart attack in his East
Hampton home on the morning of 25
September 1933.

AFTERWORD

RING

For a year and a half, the writer of this appreciation was Ring Lardner's most familiar companion; after that geography made separations and our contacts were rare. When we last saw him in 1931 he looked already like a man on his deathbed—it was terribly sad to see that six feet three inches of kindness stretched out ineffectual in the hospital room; his fingers trembled with a match, the tight skin on his handsome skull was marked as a mask of misery and nervous pain.

He gave a very different impression when I first saw him in 1921—he seemed to have an abundance of quiet vitality that would enable him to outlast anyone, to take himself for long spurts of work or play that would ruin an ordinary constitution. He had recently convulsed the country with the famous kitten-and-coat saga (it had to do with a world's series bet and with the impending conversion of some kittens into fur), and the evidence, a beautiful sable, was worn by his wife at the time. In those days he was interested in people, sports, bridge, music, the stage, the newspapers, the magazines, the books. But though I did not know it, the change in him had already begun—the impenetrable despair that dogged him for a dozen years to his death.

He had practically given up sleeping, save on short

vacations deliberately consecrated to simple pleasures, most frequently golf with his friends, Grantland Rice or John Wheeler. Many a night we talked over a case of Canadian ale until bright dawn when Ring would rise and yawn:

> "Well, I guess the children have left for school by this time—I might as well go home."

The woes of many people haunted him—for example the doctor's death sentence pronounced upon Tad, the cartoonist (who, in fact, nearly outlived Ring)—it was as if he believed he could and ought to do something about it. And as he struggled to fulfill his contracts, one of which, a comic strip based on the character of "the busher," was a terror indeed, it was obvious that he felt his work to be directionless, merely "copy." So he was inclined to turn his cosmic sense of responsibility into the channel of solving other people's problems—finding someone an introduction to a manager, placing a friend in a job, maneuvering a man into a golf club. The effort made was often out of proportion to the situation; the truth back of it was that Ring was getting off— he was a faithful and conscientious workman to the end, but he had stopped finding any fun in his work ten years before he died.

About that time (1922) a publisher undertook to reissue his old books and collect his recent stories and this gave him a sense of existing in the literary world as well as with the public, and he got some satisfaction from the reiterated statements of Mencken and F.P.A. as to his true stature as a writer. But I don't think he cared then—it is hard to understand but I don't think he really gave a damn about anything except his personal relations with people. A case in point was his attitude to those imitators who lifted everything except the shirt off his back—only Hemingway has been so thoroughly frisked—it worried the imitators more than it worried Ring. His attitude was that if they got stuck in the process he'd help them over any tough place.

Throughout this period of huge earnings and an increasingly solid reputation on top and below, there were two ambitions more important to Ring than the work by which he will be remembered: he wanted to be a musician—sometimes he dramatized himself ironically as a thwarted composer—and he wanted to write shows. His dealings with managers would make a whole story: they were always commissioning him to do work which they promptly forgot they had ordered, and accepting librettos that they never produced. Only with the aid of the practical George Kaufman did he achieve his ambition, and by then he was too far gone in illness to get a proper satisfaction from it.

The point of these paragraphs is that whatever Ring's achievement was it fell short of the achievement he was capable of, and this because of a cynical attitude toward his work. How far back did that attitude go—back to his youth in a Michigan village? Certainly back to his days with the Cubs. During those years, when most men of promise achieve an adult education, if only in the school of war, Ring moved in the company of a few dozen illiterates playing a boy's game. A boy's game, with no more possibilities in it than a boy could master, a game bounded by walls which kept out novelty or danger, change or adventure. This material, the observation of it under such circumstances, was the text of Ring's schooling during the most formative period of the mind. A writer can spin on about his adventures after thirty, after forty, after fifty, but the criteria by which these adventures are weighed and valued are irrevocably settled at the age of twenty-five. However deeply Ring might cut into it, his cake had the diameter of Frank Chance's diamond.

Here was his artistic problem, and it promised future trouble. So long as he wrote within that inclosure the result was magnificent: within it he heard and recorded the voice of a continent. But when, inevitably, he outgrew his interest in it, what was Ring left with?

He was left with his fine etymological technique—and he was left rather helpless in those few acres. He had been formed by the very world on which his hilarious irony had released itself. He had fought his way through to knowing what people's motives are and what means they are likely to resort to in order to attain their goals. He was up with the best of them, but now there was a new problem—what to do about it. He went on seeing, and the sights traveled back the optic nerve, but no longer to be thrown off in fiction, because they were no longer sights that could be weighed and valued by the old criteria. It was never that he was completely sold on athletic virtuosity as the be-all and end-all of problems; the trouble was that he could find nothing finer. Imagine life conceived as a business of beautiful muscular organization—an arising, an effort, a good break, a sweat, a bath, a meal, a sleep—imagine it achieved; then imagine trying to apply that standard to the horribly complicated mess of living where nothing, even the greatest conceptions and workings and achievements, is else but messy, spotty, tortuous—and then one can imagine the confusion that Ring faced coming out of the ball park.

He kept on recording but he no longer projected, and this accumulation, which he has taken with him to the grave, crippled his spirit in the latter years. It was not the fear of Niles, Michigan, that hampered him—it was the habit of silence formed in the presence of the "ivory" with which he lived and worked. Remember it was not humble ivory—Ring has demonstrated that—it was arrogant, imperative, often megalomaniacal ivory. He got a habit of silence, then the habit of repression that finally took the form of his odd little crusade in The New Yorker against pornographic songs. He had agreed with himself to spend only a small portion of his mind.

The present writer once suggested to him that he organize some cadre on which he could adequately display his talents, suggesting that it should be something deeply personal, and something on which Ring could take his time, but he dismissed the idea lightly; he was a disillusioned idealist but he had served his Goddess well, and no other could be casually created for him—"This is something that can be printed," he reasoned, "this, however must join that accumulated mass of reflections that can never be written."

He covered himself in such cases with protests of his inability to bring off anything big, but this was specious, for he was a proud man and had no reason to rate his abilities cheaply. He refused to "tell all" because in a crucial period of his life he had formed the habit of not doing it—and this he had elevated gradually into a standard of taste. It never satisfied him by a damn sight.

So one is haunted not only by a sense of personal loss but by a conviction that Ring got less percentage of himself on paper than any other American author of the first flight. There is "You Know Me, Al," and there are about a dozen wonderful short stories, (My God! he hadn't even saved them—the material of "How to Write Short Stories" was obtained by photographing old issues of magazines in the public library!) and there is some of the most uproarious and inspired nonsense since Lewis Carroll—the latter yet to be properly examined and edited. Most of the rest is mediocre stuff, with flashes, and I would do Ring a disservice to suggest it should be set upon an altar and worshiped, as have been the most casual relics of Mark Twain. God knows those three volumes should seem enough—to everyone who didn't know Ring. But I venture that no one who knew him but will agree that the personality of the man overlapped it. Proud, shy, solemn, shrewd, polite, brave, kind, merciful, honorable—with the affection these qualities aroused he created in addition a certain awe in people. His intentions, his will, once in motion were formidable factors in dealing with him—he always did every single thing he said he would do. Frequently he was the melancholy Jacques, and sad company indeed, but under any conditions a noble dignity flowed from him, so that time in his company always seemed well spent.

On my desk, at the moment, I have the letters that Ring wrote to us; here is a letter one thousand words long, here is one of two thousand words—theatrical gossip, literary shop talk, flashes of wit but not much wit, for he was feeling thin and saving the best of that for his work, anecdotes of his activities. I reprint the most typical one I can find:

The Dutch Treat show was a week ago Friday night. Grant Rice and I had reserved a table, and a table holds ten people and no more. Well, I had invited, as one guest, Jerry Kern, but he telephoned at the last moment that he couldn't come. I then consulted with Grant Rice, who said he had no substitute in mind, but that it was a shame to waste our extra ticket when tickets were at a premium. So I called up Jones, and Jones said yes, and would it be all right for him to bring along a former Senator who was a pal of his and had been good to him in Washington. I said I was sorry, but our table was filled and besides, we didn't have an extra ticket. "Maybe I could dig up another ticket somewhere," said Jones. "I don't believe so," I said, "but anyway the point is that we haven't room at our table." "Well," said Jones, "I could have the Senator eat somewhere else and join us in time for the show." "Yes," I said, "but we have no ticket for him." Well, what he thought up was to bring himself and the Senator and I had a hell of a time getting an extra ticket and shoving the Senator in at another table where he wasn't wanted, and later in the evening, the Senator thanked Jones and said he was the greatest fella in the world and all I got was goodnight.

Well, I must close and nibble on a carrot.
R.W.L.

Even in a telegram Ring could compress a lot of himself. Here is one:

When are you coming back and why please answer

Ring Lardner.

This is not the moment to recollect Ring's convivial aspects, especially as he had, long before his death, ceased to find amusement in dissipation, or indeed in the whole range of what is called entertainment—save for his perennial interest in songs. By grace of the radio and of the many musicians who, drawn by his enormous magnetism, made pilgrimages to his bedside, he had a consolation in the last days, and he made the most of it, hilariously rewriting Cole Porter's lyrics in The New Yorker. But it would be an evasion for the present writer not to say that when he was Ring's neighbor a decade ago, they tucked a lot under their belts in many weathers, and spent many words on many men and things. At no time did I feel that I had known him enough, or that anyone knew him—it was not the feeling that there was more stuff in him and that it should come out, it was rather a qualitative difference, it was rather as though, due to some inadequacy in one's self, one had not penetrated to something unsolved, new and unsaid. That is why one wishes that Ring had written down a larger proportion of what was in his mind and heart. It would have saved him longer for us, and that in itself would be something. But I would like to know what it was, and now I will go on wishing—what did Ring want, how did he want things to be, how did he think things were?

A great and good American is dead. Let us not obscure him by the flowers, but walk up and look at that fine medallion, all torn by sorrows that perhaps we are not equipped to understand. Ring made no enemies, because he was kind, and to many millions he gave release and delight.

F. Scott Fitzgerald

—from *The New Republic,*
11 October 1933,
pp. 254-55

A CHRONOLOGICAL LISTING

RING LARDNER'S BOOKS

Books

ZANZIBAR: A COMIC OPERA IN TWO ACTS. Niles, Mich.: Fred D. Cook, 1903.

MARCH 6TH; THE HOME COMING OF CHARLES A. COMISKEY, JOHN J. MCGRAW, AND JAMES J. CALLAHAN. Chicago: Blakely Printing Co., 1914. With Edward C. Heeman.

BIB BALLADS. Chicago: P. F. Volland & Co., 1915.

YOU KNOW ME AL. New York: George H. Doran Co., 1916

GULLIBLE'S TRAVELS. Indianapolis: Bobbs-Merrill Co., 1917

TREAT 'EM ROUGH. Indianapolis: Bobbs-Merrill Co., 1918

MY FOUR WEEKS IN FRANCE. Indianapolis: Bobbs-Merrill Co., 1918

REGULAR FELLOWS I HAVE MET. Chicago: Wilmot, 1919

OWN YOUR OWN HOME. Indianapolis: Bobbs-Merrill Co., 1919

THE REAL DOPE. Indianapolis: Bobbs-Merrill Co., 1919

THE YOUNG IMMIGRUNTS. Indianapolis: Bobbs-Merrill Co., 1920

THE BIG TOWN. Indianapolis: Bobbs-Merrill Co., 1921

SYMPTOMS OF BEING 35. Indianapolis: Bobbs-Merrill Co., 1921

SAY IT WITH OIL. New York: George H. Doran Co., 1923

HOW TO WRITE SHORT STORIES. New York: Charles Scribner's Sons, 1924

WHAT OF IT? New York: Charles Scribner's Sons, 1925

THE LOVE NEST AND OTHER STORIES. New York: Charles Scribner's Sons, 1926

THE STORY OF A WONDER MAN. New York: Charles Scribner's Sons, 1927

ROUND UP. New York: Charles Scribner's Sons, 1929

JUNE MOON. New York: Charles Scribner's Sons, 1930. With George S. Kaufman.

LOSE WITH A SMILE. New York: Charles Scribner's Sons, 1933

FIRST AND LAST. New York: Charles Scribner's Sons, 1934. Ed. Gilbert Seldes.

OF FIRST PUBLICATIONS OF

AND MAGAZINE PIECES

Stories and Articles

Magazine pieces which appeared in books are designated by the following abbreviations, in parentheses, of the books in which they were first collected:

YKMA—You Know Me Al
GT—Gullible's Travels
TER—Treat 'em Rough
MFWIF—My Four Weeks in France
OYOH—Own Your Own Home
TRD—The Real Dope
TBT—The Big Town
SIWO—Say It With Oil
HTWSS—How To Write Short Stories
WOI—What of It?
LN—The Love Nest
RU—Round Up
LWAS—Lose With a Smile
FL—First and Last

1912

"The Cost of Baseball" (article). *Collier's,* March 2.

1914

"A Busher's Letters Home" (story). *Saturday Evening Post,* March 7 **(YKMA).**
"My Roomy" (story). *Saturday Evening Post,* May 9 **(HTWSS).**

"The Busher Comes Back" (story). *Saturday Evening Post,* May 23 **(YKMA).**

"The Busher's Honeymoon" (story). *Saturday Evening Post,* July 11 **(YKMA).**

"Sick 'Em" (story). *Saturday Evening Post,* July 25.

"Horseshoes" (story). *Saturday Evening Post,* August 15 **(HTWSS).**

"A New Busher Breaks In" (story). *Saturday Evening Post,* September 12 **(YKMA).**

"The Busher's Kid" (story). *Saturday Evening Post,* October 3 **(YKMA).**

"The Busher Beats It Hence" (story). *Saturday Evening Post,* November 7 **(YKMA).**

"Back to Baltimore" (story). *Redbook,* November.

1915

"Tour No. 2" (story in two parts). *Saturday Evening Post,* February 13, 20.

"Own Your Own Home" (story). *Redbook,* January **(OYOH).**

"The Busher Abroad" (story in four parts). *Saturday Evening Post,* March 20, April 10, May 8, 15.

" 'Braves' Is Right" (article). *American,* March.

"Some Team" (article). *American,* April.

"Welcome to Our City" (story). *Redbook,* May **(OYOH).**

"Tyrus" (article). *American,* June.

"The Busher's Welcome Home" (story). *Saturday Evening Post,* June 5.

"The Last Laugh" (story). *Redbook,* July **(OYOH).**

"Alibi Ike" (story). *Saturday Evening Post,* July 31 **(HTWSS).**

"Matty" (article). *American,* August.

"Harmony" (story). *McClure's,* August **(HTWSS).**

"Uncivil War" (story). *Redbook,* September **(OYOH).**

"The Poor Simp" (story). *Saturday Evening Post,* September 11.

"Where Do You Get That Noise?" (story). *Saturday Evening Post,* October 23.

"Oh, You Bonehead" (story). *Saturday Evening Post,* October 30.

1916

"Carmen" (story). *Saturday Evening Post,* February 19 **(GT).**

"Three Kings and a Pair" (story). *Saturday Evening Post*, March 11 **(GT)**.

"Good for the Soul" (story). *Saturday Evening Post*, March 25.

"War Bribes" (story). *Redbook*, April.

"The Crook" (story). *Saturday Evening Post*, June 24.

"The Swift Six" (story). *Redbook*, July.

"Gullible's Travels" (story). *Saturday Evening Post*, August 19 **(GT)**.

"Champion" (story). *Metropolitan*, October **(HTWSS)**.

"The Water Cure" (story). *Saturday Evening Post*, October 14 **(GT)**.

"A One-Man Team" (story). *Redbook*, November.

1917

"The Facts" (story) *Metropolitan*, January **(HTWSS)**.

"Three Without, Doubled" (story). *Saturday Evening Post*, January 13 **(GT)**.

"Tour-Y-10" (story). *Metropolitan*, February.

"The Hold-Out" (story). *Saturday Evening Post*, March 24.

"Ring Lardner—Himself" (autobiographical). *Saturday Evening Post*, April 28.

"Fore!" (story). *Redbook*, May.

"A Friendly Game" (story). *Saturday Evening Post*, May 5.

"Ball-A-Hole" (story). *Saturday Evening Post*, May 12.

"The Yellow Kid" (story). *Saturday Evening Post*, June 23.

"A Reporter's Diary" (article in eight parts). *Collier's*, September 29, October 13, November 3, November 17, December 1, December 15, 1917; January 12, January 19, 1918 **(MFWIF)**.

"The Last Night" (story). *Redbook*, November.

1918

"The Clubby Roadster" (story). *Redbook*, February.

"Call for Mr. Keefe" (story). *Saturday Evening Post*, March 9.

"Jack the Kaiser Killer" (story). *Saturday Evening Post*, March 23. **(TER)**

"Corporal Punishment" (story). *Saturday Evening Post*, April 13 **(TER)**.

"Purls before Swine" (story). *Saturday Evening Post,* June 8 **(TER).**
"And Many a Stormy Wind Shall Blow" (story). *Saturday Evening Post,* July 6 **(TRD).**
"Private Valentine" (story). *Saturday Evening Post,* August 3 **(TRD).**
"Stragety and Tragedy" (story). *Saturday Evening Post,* August 31 **(TRD).**
"A Chip of the Old Block" (story). *Redbook,* September.
"Decorated" (story). *Saturday Evening Post,* October 26 **(TRD).**
"Sammy Boy" (story). *Saturday Evening Post,* December 21 **(TRD).**

1919

"Simple Simon" (story). *Saturday Evening Post,* January 25 **(TRD).**
"The Busher Reenlists" (story). *Saturday Evening Post,* April 19.
"The Battle of Texas" (story). *Saturday Evening Post,* May 24.
"Along Came Ruth" (story). *Saturday Evening Post,* July 26.
"The Courtship of T. Dorgan" (story). *Saturday Evening Post,* September 6.
"The Busher Pulls a Mays" (story). *Saturday Evening Post,* October 13.

1920

"The Young Immigrunts" (story). *Saturday Evening Post,* January 31 **(TYI).**
"Quick Returns" (story). *Saturday Evening Post,* March 27 **(TBT).**
"Beautiful Katie" (story). *Saturday Evening Post,* July 10 **(TBT).**
"The Battle of Long Island" (story). *Saturday Evening Post,* November 27 **(TBT).**

1921

"Only One" (story). *Saturday Evening Post,* February 12 **(TBT).**
"What Is the 'American Language'?" (review). *Bookman,* March.
"General Symptoms of Being 35" (article). *American,* May **(WOI).**
"The Comic" (story). *Saturday Evening Post,* May 14 **(TBT).**
"A Frame-Up" (story). *Saturday Evening Post,* June 18 **(HTWSS).**

"Some Like Them Cold" (story). *Saturday Evening Post*, October 21 **(HTWSS).**

"The Battle of the Century" (story). *Saturday Evening Post*, October 29.

1922

"East Is East and Michigan Is Michigan When It Comes to Dogs" (article). *Wheeler's Magazine*, February.

"A Caddy's Diary" (story). *Saturday Evening Post*, March 11 **(HTWSS).**

"The Golden Honeymoon" (story). *Cosmopolitan*, July **(HTWSS).**

"The Bull Pen" (play). *Judge*, July 29.

"My Week in Cuba" (article). *Cosmopolitan*, August.

"You Know Me, Al" (miscellany). *Cosmopolitan*, September.

"For He's a Jolly Good Fellow" (article). *Cosmopolitan*, October.

"Let's Go!" (article). *Cosmopolitan*, November.

"Say It With Oil" (article). *American*, November **(SIWO).**

"Little Sunbeams of Success" (article). *Cosmopolitan*, December.

"What I Don't Know about Horses" (article). *Trotter and Pacer*, December.

1923

"Not Guilty" (play). *Cosmopolitan*, January.

"Bringing Up Children" (article). *Cosmopolitan*, February.

"The Dames" (article). *Hearst's International*, March **(WOI).**

"Why Authors?" (article). *Hearst's International*, April **(WOI).**

"In Regards to Geniuses" (article). *Hearst's International*, May **(WOI).**

"The Big Drought" (article). *Hearst's International*, June **(WOI).**

"Enoch Arden" (article). *Bookman*, June.

"Bedtime Stories (How to Tell a Princess and Bluebeard)" (article). *Hearst's International*, July **(WOI).**

"Cinderella" (article). *Hearst's International*, August **(WOI).**

"What I Ought to of Learnt in High School" (article). *American*, November.

1924

"I Gaspiri" (play). *Chicago Literary Times*, February 15 **(WOI)**.
"The Lardner Plan" (article), *Life*, March 20.
"A Close-Up of Domba Splew" (article). *Hearst's International*, June **(WOI)**.
"What of It?" (article). *Liberty*, June 7 **(WOI)**.
"In Conference" (article). *Liberty*, August 16 **(WOI)**.

1925

"The Other Side" (article in five parts). *Liberty*, February 14, February 21, February 28, March 7, March 14 **(WOI)**.
"Haircut" (story). *Liberty*, March 28 **(LN)**.
"Mr. and Mrs. Fix-It" (story). *Liberty*, May 9 **(LN)**.
"Sea Island Sports" (article). *American Golfer*, May 16.
"What You Will Encounter in Nassau" (article). *American Golfer*, May 30.
"Cora, or Fun at a Spa" (play). *Vanity Fair*, June **(FL)**.
"Zone of Quiet" (story). *Cosmopolitan*, June **(LN)**.
"Women" (story). *Liberty*, June 20 **(LN)**.
"The Love Nest" (story). *Cosmopolitan*, August **(LN)**.
"A Day with Conrad Green" (story). *Liberty*, October 3 **(LN)**.
"Reunion" (story). *Liberty*, October 31 **(LN)**.

1926

"Who Dealt?" (story). *Cosmopolitan*, January **(LN)**.
"Rhythm" (story). *Cosmopolitan*, March **(LN)**.
"Travelogue" (story). *Cosmopolitan*, May **(RU)**.
"I Can't Breathe" (story). *Cosmopolitan*, September **(RU)**.
"The Jade Necklace" (story). *Cosmopolitan*, November.

1927

"Sun Cured" (story). *Cosmopolitan*, January **(RU)**.
"Hurry Kane" (story). *Cosmopolitan*, May **(RU)**.
"Now and Then" (story). *Cosmopolitan*, June **(RU)**.

"The Spinning Wheel" (story). *Cosmopolitan*, July.

"Dinner Bridge" (play). *New Republic*, July 20 **(FL)**.

"The Venomous Viper of the Volga" (story). *Cosmopolitan*, September.

"Miss Sawyer, Champion" (article). *New Yorker*, September 10 **(FL)**.

"Man Not Overboard" (story). *Cosmopolitan*, November **(RU)**.

1928

"Anniversary" (story). *Cosmopolitan*, January **(RU)**.

"Nora" (story). *Cosmopolitan*, February **(RU)**.

"Liberty Hall" (story). *Cosmopolitan*, March **(RU)**.

"The Battle of Palm Beach" (article). *Collier's*, March 24.

"There Are Smiles" (story). *Cosmopolitan*, April **(RU)**.

"With Rod and Gun" (article). *Collier's*, April 7.

"Mr. Frisbie" (story). *Cosmopolitan*, June **(RU)**.

"Laugh, Clown!" (article). *Collier's*, June 23.

"Wedding Day" (story). *Cosmopolitan*, July.

"Dante and———" (article). *New Yorker*, July 7 **(FL)**.

"The Maysville Minstrel" (story). *Cosmopolitan*, September **(RU)**.

"Dinner" (story). *Harper's Bazaar*, September **(RU)**.

"Just Politics" (article in two parts). *Collier's*, September 1 and September 15.

"Can You Keep a Secret" (article). *Collier's*, October 6.

"Ex Parte" (story). *Cosmopolitan*, November **(RU)**.

1929

"Old Folks' Christmas" (story). *Cosmopolitan*, January **(RU)**.

"Adrift in New York" (article). *Collier's*, January 12.

"With Rope and Gum" (article). *Collier's*, February 2.

"Onward and Upward" (article). *Collier's*, February 16.

"Absent Minded Beggar" (story). *Cosmopolitan*, March.

"Contract" (story). *Harper's Bazaar*, March **(RU)**.

"Boy Entertainer" (article). *Collier's*, March 2.

"Pluck and Luck" (article). *Collier's*, March 16.

"Paul the Fiddler" (article). *Collier's*, March 23.

"Reuben, the Young Artist" (article). *Collier's*, April 13.

"Keeper of the Bees" (article). *Collier's*, May 11.

"High Rollers" (story). *Cosmopolitan,* June.
"Ringside Seat" (article). *Collier's,* June 16.
"Stop Me If You've Heard This One" (story). *Cosmopolitan,* July.
"Why We Have Left Hands" (article). *Collier's,* July 6.
"Tee Time" (article). *Collier's,* July 27.
"Oh, Shoot!" (article). *Collier's,* August 10.
"Nice Quiet Racket" (article). *Collier's,* August 31.
"Pity Is Akin" (story). *Cosmopolitan,* September.
"Bad News for Pitchers" (article). *Collier's,* September 14.
"Large Coffee" (article). *New Yorker,* September 28 **(FL)**.
"Any Ice Today, Lady" (article). *Collier's,* September 28.
"Cubs Win World Series" (article). *Collier's,* October 12.
"That Old Sweetheart of Mine" (story). *Cosmopolitan,* November.
"Jersey City Gendarmerie, Je T'aime" (article). *New Yorker,* November 2.
"Army Black and Navy Blue" (article). *Collier's,* November 30.
"Great Blessings" (story). *Cosmopolitan,* December.
"Bobby or Bust" (article). *Collier's,* December 21.

1930

"Second-Act Curtain" (article). *Collier's,* April 19.
"Sit Still" (article). *New Yorker,* April 19.
"Mamma" (story). *Good Housekeeping,* June,
"X-Ray" (article). *New Yorker,* July 15.
"Words and Music" (story). *Good Housekeeping,* August.
"Bre'er Rabbit Ball" (article). *New Yorker,* September 13.
"Asleep on the Deep" (article). *New Yorker,* October 4.
"Tables for Two" (article). *New Yorker,* October 18.
"The Higher-Ups" (article). *New Yorker,* November 1.
"From a Zealous Non-Worker" (article). *New Yorker,* November 29.

1931

"Old Man Liver" (article). *New Yorker,* January 3 **(FL)**.
"Cured!" (story). *Redbook,* March.
"Insomnia" (story). *Cosmopolitan,* May.
"All Quiet on the Eastern Front" (article). *New Yorker,* June 27.
"A Slow Train through Arizona" (article). *Cosmopolitan,* September.

"Meet Mr. Howley" (autobiographical). *Saturday Evening Post,* November 14.

"Me, Boy Scout" (autobiographical). *Saturday Evening Post,* November 21.

"Quandroon" (play). *New Yorker,* December 19 **(FL).**

1932

"Caught in the Draft" (autobiographical). *Saturday Evening Post,* January 9.

"Heap Big Chief" (autobiographical). *Saturday Evening Post,* January 23.

"Chicago's Beau Monde" (autobiographical). *Saturday Evening Post,* February 20.

"Alias James Clarkson" (autobiographical). *Saturday Evening Post,* April 16.

"One Hit, One Error, One Left" (story). *Saturday Evening Post,* April 23 **(LWAS).**

"When the Moon Comes over the Mountain" (story). *Saturday Evening Post,* May 7 **(LWAS).**

"Lose with a Smile" (story). *Saturday Evening Post,* June 11 **(LWAS).**

"Over the Waves" (radio review). *New Yorker,* June 18.

"Heavy Da-Dee-Dough Boys" (radio review). *New Yorker,* June 25.

"The Truth about Ruth" (radio review). *New Yorker,* July 2.

"Meet Me in St. Louie" (story). *Saturday Evening Post,* July 2 **(LWAS).**

"The Crooner's Paradise" (radio review). *New Yorker,* July 16.

"Allie Bobs Oop Again" (radio review). *New Yorker,* July 30.

"Holycaust" (story). *Saturday Evening Post,* July 30 **(LWAS).**

"Deacon Gets Tilt for Tat" (radio review). *New Yorker,* August 20.

"An Epistle of Paul" (radio review). *New Yorker,* September 3.

"The Ides of June" (story). *Saturday Evening Post,* September 5 **(LWAS).**

"Life of the Boswells" (radio review). *New Yorker,* September 17.

"Pu-leese! Mr. Hemingway" (radio review). *New Yorker,* October 1.

"The Crucial Game" (radio review). *New Yorker,* October 22.

"Eckie" (article). *Saturday Evening Post,* October 22.

"The Lor and the Profits" (article). *American Spectator,* November.

"Ring Lardner Explains Why He Will Vote Socialist" (article). *New Leader,* November 5.

"Herb and Frank Panic 'Em" (radio review). *New Yorker*, November 5.

"Lyricists Strike Pay Dirt" (radio review). *New Yorker*, November 19.

"Announcer's Prep School" (radio review). *New Yorker*, December 3.

"Some Short-Selling" (radio review). *New Yorker*, December 17.

1933

"Ring In! (Two Weeks Late)" (radio review). *New Yorker*, January 14.

"Rudy in Irate Mood" (radio review). *New Yorker*, February 4.

"An Infant Industry" (radio review). *New Yorker*, February 25.

"I Am a Fugitive from a National Network" (radio review). *New Yorker*, March 18.

"The Old Man Shows His Air Mail" (radio review). *New Yorker*, April 8.

"We're All Sisters under the Hide of Me" (radio review). *New Yorker*, May 6.

"Hail to the Chief" (radio review). *New Yorker*, May 27.

"Some Champions" (article). *Saturday Evening Post*, June 3.

"Radio's All-America Team for 1932-1933" (radio review). *New Yorker*, June 17.

"Comics Face Starvation as Gag Men Near Wits' End" (radio review). *New Yorker*, July 8.

"Ricordi to the Rescue" (radio review). *New Yorker*, August 5.

"The Perfect Radio Program" (radio review). *New Yorker*, August 26.

"Take a Walk" (story). *American*, October.

"Odd's Bodkins" (article). *New Yorker*, October 7 **(FL)**.

"Bob's Birthday" (story). *Redbook*, November.

1934

"Poodle" (story). *Delineator*, January.

"Via the Canal" (story). *New York Sunday News*, January 7.

"Greek Tragedy" (story). *Esquire*, February.

1935

"Widow" (story). *Redbook,* October.
"Freedom of the Press" (story). *Pictorial Review,* November.
"How Are You?" (story). *Redbook,* December.

1936

"Christmas Card, 1929" (verse). *Reader's Digest,* January.

1954

"Claude Diphthong, Student of Crime" (story). *Ellery Queen's Mystery Magazine,* August.

Contributions to Books

"Baseball—American" and "Ham—American," H. L. Mencken, THE AMERICAN LANGUAGE. 2nd ed. New York: Knopf, 1921.

"Sport and Play," CIVILIZATION IN THE UNITED STATES. New York: Harcourt, Brace & Co., 1922. Ed. Harold Stearns.

"Autobiographical Sketch," "Inside Facts of the Writing Game," and "A Small Vocabulary May Have a Big Kick," Thomas L. Masson, OUR AMERICAN HUMORISTS. New York: Dodd, Mead & Co., 1922.

"Introduction," H. T. Webster, THE TIMID SOUL. New York: Simon & Schuster, 1931.

"Foreword," THE SIXTH NEW YORKER ALBUM. New York: Harper & Bros., 1933.

"Foreword," BARBER SHOP BALLADS AND HOW TO SING THEM. New York: Prentice-Hall, 1940. Ed. Sigmund Spaeth.

"On Conversation," A SUBTREASURY OF AMERICAN HUMOR. New York: Coward-McCann, Inc., 1941. Ed. E. B. White and Katherine S. White.

INDEX